Rhythm
of a
Captured
Heart

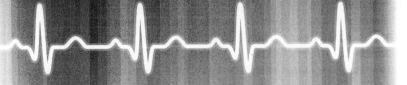

John Brown

OASIS HOUSE
GRANDVIEW, MISSOURI

Rhythm of a Captured Heart
Copyright © 2011 John E. Brown
Published by Oasis House
PO Box 522
Grandview, MO 64030-0522

www.oasishouse.com

To contact the author:
www.johnbrownspen.com
Email: johnbrownspen@gmail.com

Unless otherwise noted all scriptures quoted are from the New American Standard Bible.

Scripture quotations taken from the New American Standard Bible ®, Copyright © 1960, 1962, 1963, 1968, 1971, 1972, 1973, 1975, 1977, 1995 by The Lockman Foundation. Used by permission. (www.Lockman.org)

Scripture quotations taken from the Amplified ® Bible, Copyright © 1954, 1958, 1962, 1964, 1965, 1987 by The Lockman Foundation. Used by permission. (www.Lockman.org)

Scripture quotations taken from the 21st Century King James Version ®, copyright © 1994. Used by permission of Deuel Enterprises, Inc., Gary, SD 57237. All rights reserved.

Edited by Jackie Macgirvin and Meg Massey.

All rights reserved. This book or parts thereof may not be reproduced in any form, except for brief quotations in reviews, without the written permission from the publisher.

Printed in the United States of America
ISBN: 978-0-9826018-3-9

Cathy & Jim,
God's Richest blessings
to you!
John

Endorsements

John Brown is the kind of person and the kind of teacher that sneaks up on you and gets into your heart and head with barely an invitation. I think it's because he's a "blue collar" kind of guy whose noble-like spiritual gift of hearing from and speaking for our Heavenly Father tends to catch you off guard. And though he could be boastful about many things he has accomplished in Christ's name, he still doesn't think too highly of himself. That is refreshing.

John is not bogged down with the kind of image creation and management that so many "celebrity" types of leaders get caught up into in our culture. He doesn't give a rip about making a reputation for himself. For many years now he has just consistently loved and served and led others (from every station of life and across the racial lines that people tend to draw) with a fiery heart full of wisdom, knowledge, first-hand experience, humility and tenderness. John is straight and true...like a well-crafted arrow from God's quiver that loves to be firmly grasped by such a Hand and shot from such a Royal Bow.

John is an effective pastor and leader. John is also a great teacher and that is why I am so excited about *Rhythm of a Captured Heart*. John is a practitioner of what he preaches. His illustrations are well-chosen. He has rare insight into all kinds of passages from Scripture. He tells a great story. He is *real* and his words are timely, persuasive and endearing. His teaching is...well...clean and empowering. Added to all of this, John is one of the most witty and humorous guys I am privileged to know. John Brown is simply delightful and so is his book. Please read and savor it and pass it on to your friends.

Michael Sullivant, author, speaker, spiritual director
Kansas City, Missouri

I have had the honor of knowing John Brown and his dear wife for many years. We have both served the Lord through good times and hard ones. John's writings do not come from theory; they come from life's lessons. Therefore, I consider it a privilege to commend to you *Rhythm of a Captured Heart* by John E. Brown. You will learn about times of grace, times of faith, times to race, and times to rest and when to leave it all in His great big, yet personal capable hands. It is with joy that I commend the message and the messenger for such a time as this.

James W. Goll, Franklin, Tennessee
Encounters Network & Prayer Storm & Compassion Acts
author of *The Seer, The Lost Art of Intercession, Deliverance from Darkness, The Coming Israel Awakening* and many more.

In a world of chaos, distractions, and sin, it isn't difficult to miss the heart and the voice of God. In this book, Pastor John Brown invites readers to pursue a life that pulsates with the rhythm of a captured heart, a heart in tune with the Spirit of God. Using examples from his own life, as well as the experiences of Biblical figures, Pastor John demonstrates the love of a God who longs to use His people, despite imperfections and past mistakes. Every chapter provides practical methods and Biblical truths that will not only provide a road map to the very heart of God, but encouragement to continue living our daily lives completely captured by God's grace.

Meg Massey, editor
Wyomissing, Pennsylvania
www.creative.megmassey.com

Special Thanks

To my wife Kathie. I would not be in the Kingdom unless God sent you to me. None of the encounters with God that this book describes would exist without you.

To Rachel, Jenny, George, Monty, Sam, Emma, Reagan, Paxton and Olivia. You are the best family anyone could ever hope for.

To James Harris, Roger Hanson, Tim Gerdts and Doug Day, my elder team, you guys are amazing.

To Barbara Squires, my ministry assistant, your loyal and faithful work is a tremendous blessing and help to me.

To the "Saturday Prayer Group" at Harmony. Your affirmation of me and confirmation of my thoughts and ideas have been a mainstay for me. To Scott and Cyndie Belke and Sara Bailey, your intercession and prayer involvement for this project have served as a magnet, pulling and empowering me onward.

To Jackie Macgirvin and Meg Massey, thank you for your editorial help.

To Dale Jimmo, thank you for your excellent work.

To Eric Jessen, thanks for your sensitivity and professionalism in creating the cover design.

To Cyndie Belke, thank you for seeing and drawing my heart.

To Bob Sorge and Oasis House, thank you for building bridges for me.

To the Lord Jesus Christ, for choosing such an unlikely and undeserving one to be included in your Kingdom.

Table of Contents

Introduction

Nothing on this earth is more significant than having a vibrant and satisfying relationship with God. Do you, or those you know, enjoy a consistently vital prayer life? Wouldn't it be wonderful if more of the church experienced the fruitfulness of abiding in the life of God and having His Spirit abiding in them?

This book is all about our God revealing Himself to us and inviting us into the wonderful rhythm of life in His Spirit. The Lord has so graciously worked with me and has used all sorts of things to help me see His heart for those who belong to Him.

You will find a number of life-experiences and Biblical insights that reveal God's heart in these pages. You will also find some very practical "take-aways" that can truly help you to know Him better and love Him more deeply. The Lord's desire for us is to know Him intimately and for us to live in a present-tense moment to moment reality with Him. The Bible tells us that our life is "hidden with Christ in God!" (Colossians 3:3) This book is filled with descriptions of how to discover and develop that truth in our life in everyday ways.

My hope is that my personal encounters with the Spirit of God and the Biblical "nuggets" that I have included here will increase your capacity to walk with God at a higher level. I pray that the word pictures that I have painted will open doors and answer questions for you. My desire is that you will receive some more "pieces" to the puzzle and that you will be energized to press on to all the purposes of God for your life.

My heart for you is that God will take the details of my story and make them empowered discoveries for you and those you may minister to. May God tune your heart with the refreshing rhythm of Heaven!

1

The Cadence of the Capture

The air was crisp and the sky was clear and brilliant in the autumn sun. A myriad of colors painted the trees as their leaves rustled in the breeze. It was fall and the changing of the seasons was wonderful to behold. But other breezes were blowing and other seasons were emerging as well. I was in the middle of preaching a series called "The Fire of God." I was deeply stirred about God's passion for His church when He whispered a phrase to me which I began to release back to Him in prayer. "O Lord, I want my life to pulsate with the 'rhythm of a captured heart.'" I spoke those words and prayed that phrase with real passion and desire but as I soon discovered, with very little understanding.

I have pursued the Lord about the rhythm of a captured heart and I invite you to explore with me what it means and how we can live before Him with a heart like that. Jesus reveals a tremendous truth to us about His disposition of heart toward the Father in John 14:30-31. *"I will not speak much more with you, for the ruler of the world is coming and he has nothing in Me; but so that the world may know that I love the Father, I do exactly as the Father commanded Me."* It took me several years to come to an understanding of Jesus' words but when light broke through from this passage my heart was dramatically changed.

I had been saved for five or six years and I was serving

as the youth pastor of a small Baptist church. My heart was
stirred for God but I felt *stuck,* so I decided to pray and fast
for a day to find God's heart for my future. Fasting was a new
experience for me, and fasting for a *whole day* was equally un-
charted territory. I went to a beautiful park before sunrise and
purposed to stay there until I heard from God.

I was discouraged, hungry and grumpy, and I had a head-
ache. My watch told me that it was past 4:00 p.m. and still no
word from God. I re-affirmed my resolution not to give up until I heard from Him. Suddenly my eyes fell on John 14:31, *"But
so that the world may know that I love the Father, I do exactly as the
Father commanded Me."*

Wow! I got it. I recognized the M.O. by which Jesus had
worked. Everything that He did, every act of obedience was
to prove to the world that He loved God. My approach had
always been to try to prove to people that God loved them
(Which of course He does). This was *not* the primary rhythm of
Jesus' heart. When people saw the love Jesus had for the Father
they wanted to love Him too and were awakened to His deep
affection for them. He lived to prove how much He loved God,
and the inevitable result was people feeling loved by God.

I promised to never stand before a group of people again
without this being my primary motive. A heart abandoned to
be a lover of God is a heart in synch with Heaven's heart. I
rejoiced at the power of this truth and celebrated by breaking
my fast at Baskin-Robbins—rocky road, two scoops! My heart
was beating with the life and rhythm of Jesus' Spirit within me.
"Oh God, give us this heart—the rhythm of a captured heart!"

Let's look at some Biblical examples—David, Josiah and
Paul.

In Acts 13:22 we find these familiar words, *"I have found David the son of Jesse a man after my heart, who will do all My will."* I
love how real the Bible is and how amazing the heart of God is
toward us. This quote was written long after David's death so
everyone knew all about his life and his exploits. In fact, David
is the subject of one of the Bible's most incredible statements.
*"But for David's sake the Lord his God gave him a lamp in Jerusalem;
because David did what was right in the sight of the Lord, and had
not turned aside from anything that He commanded him all the days
of his life, except in the case of Uriah the Hittite"* (1 Kings 15:4-5).

David did all of the will of God. David also did some things outside the will of God, but he had genuine passion and commitment for God. His heart became so captured and so in synch with God that these words were written about him.

I am not talking about a sinless heart. The rhythm of a captured heart is blameless, not sinless. It is a heart that is humble before God, cleansed by the blood of Jesus and attuned to His word. David made some devastating mistakes and some horrible choices, but he responded to God's conviction and lived with the consequences of his actions in a manner that released his heart to God and God's heart to him in wonderful ways.

Let this be an encouragement to you. God is not depending upon you to be perfect. He wants you to depend on Him. A captured heart recognizes its own lack of dependability and completely depends upon the Lord. This dependence and humble reliance upon the heart of God are what helps establish this rhythm in our hearts. David had proved his dependability (actually his lack thereof) and was convinced of his need to be synchronized with Heaven's heart.

Josiah is another whose heart beat as one with the Lord's heart. We read in 2 Kings 23:25, *"Before him there was no king like him who turned to the Lord with all his heart and with all his soul and with all his might, according to all the law of Moses; nor did any like him arise after him."*

Wow! Josiah was whole-heartedly living before God, and the entire nation was blessed because of it. He responded to the Lord without reservation and brought revival to God's people. Josiah's heart response to God impacted a whole nation. God touched his heart, and he responded by tearing down altars and restoring uprightness to worship and everyday life for God's people. He restored a rhythm of godliness to his generation. This is an awesome and inspiring story that has encouraged many through the years. Something happened to Josiah's heart; an encounter with the God of the Universe that empowered him to live and think and choose differently. He lived in a league with the heart of Heaven.

We could not discuss a captured heart without including Paul. His heart resonated with Heaven's heartbeat. He knew God in marvelous ways, and he made so many powerful statements to direct us to live in the same way. I find these words to be so astounding, *"For the love of Christ controls us, having concluded this, that one died for all, therefore all died; and He died for all, so that they who live might no longer live for themselves, but for Him who died and rose again on their behalf"* (2 Corinthians 5:14-15).

Paul was constrained by God's love. He did what he did because a new love had been birthed in him, creating a new energy and rhythm of life that coursed through him. This new life, this new love, gave him grace to restrain himself from that which he needed to avoid and it empowered him to do all God desired him to do.

He had a love from God, *for* God and a love *within* him for others that gave him a connection with the upward call. He was filled with a compassion for those around him that enabled him to be abased or abound, to live free or imprisoned, to be accepted or rejected, to be honored or humiliated and to be in plenty or in want. He had a divine rhythm of life beating in his heart and he literally did do all things through Jesus who strengthened him. The love of God controlled his heart and constrained his thoughts, words and deeds. His heart simply couldn't not love. Every fiber of his being yielded to the love of God, and his heart was re-aligned and infused with Heaven's power and purpose. Paul was a man whose life was regulated by a metronome others could not hear or see.

There are several symptoms that establish a captured heart's rhythm, and help us to see how a captured heart functions. I trust that God's Spirit will use the following chapters to establish or reestablish them in you as we continue this journey together.

2

A Heart That God Can Touch

Watchman Nee tells a story about a man who had experienced a broken back and had gone through a great deal of pain. No one had to slap him on the back to get his attention, for just the slightest touch captured his undivided attention. We must pursue a heart that is sensitive to God's touch. A heart that is easily touched by God is part of that synchronization, part of establishing that captured heart rhythm with Him.

When Saul was publicly appointed king by Samuel we find these intriguing words: *"Saul also went to his house at Gibeah; and the valiant men whose hearts God touched went with him"* (1 Samuel 10:26).

Only the men whose hearts were open to God's touch rallied to the king's cause. There is a strong lesson for us here. Don't you want the Lord to nudge your heart to agree with what He is saying and doing? Don't you want to be freed from your own agenda and unsanctified opinions, and be free to cooperate with what God's Spirit is doing in your life and in our day? Ask Him to nurture a touchable heart in you. Cry out for Him to make you aware of His choice and His purpose for you, so you can be aware of what He is doing in your life. The next verse of 1 Samuel 10 is very telling, *"But certain worthless men said, 'How can this one deliver us?' And they despised him and did not bring him any present. But he kept silent"* (1 Samuel 10:27).

God was touching people's hearts. He wanted to touch them so that they could co-agree and co-labor with Him, but many did not like His man or His method, so they opposed what He was doing. Don't put yourself in that place. Do not let a hardened or untouchable heart place you in opposition to the moving of God in your life. No opinion, evaluation, tradition or position is worth being opposed to God's will.

We see a much different response in Acts 16:14, *"A woman named Lydia, from the city of Thyatira, a seller of purple fabrics and a worshipper of God, was listening."* The Lord opened her heart to respond to the things spoken by Paul. She was a worshipper and she was listening. Her heart was touchable and was opened by the Lord to the Gospel. She was led to play an intricate part in Paul's ministry in Europe. God began to capture her heart and establish the rhythm of a worshipful obedience to His presence within her.

A captured heart is one that is easily moved by the things that move God's heart. This is not just an emotional response or a twinge of pity or compassion. God touched the hearts of the men who came to support the cause of the king, and He opened Lydia's heart.

He wants your heart touchable and easily opened to Him because He wants you to champion every purpose of the King of kings. He wants you to be able to hear the word of the Lord and have the right response.

Saul's valiant men were indispensable to his ruling Israel. Paul's ministry brought salvation to Lydia's household and Lydia was a great benefactor of Paul's ministry. It is vital that we support the cause of our King and essential that we receive and respond to the word of the Lord, so we will have a heart that God can touch.

Nearly 30 years ago the Holy Spirit highlighted this verse to me: Zephaniah 3:18, *"I will gather those who grieve about the appointed feasts—they came from you, O Zion; the reproach of exile is a burden on them."* There were those in Israel who had their heart-rhythm interrupted, spiritually speaking, by their long and cruel exile in Babylon. They grieved about not being able to celebrate the feasts and fully obey God's edicts. The reproach of their exile was a burden to them. There was no "business as usual" mentality. Exile, and the reasons for their captivity weighed them down. They felt a little bit of what God's heart was feeling about His people's disobedience and estrangement from Him and their homeland. They could not simply smile and go on because God was allowing them to be touched by that which was touching Him.

When your heart is touched like this, He is able to deeply impact you with the desire of His heart - restoration! He can grace you to have the desired response, which could be intercession, grief, repentance, praise, warfare, etc. A heart that God can touch is one that will doubtless be used to touch others. Don't you want a heart like that?

Have you ever wondered or marveled at the oneness of heart exemplified in the Book of Acts? These are startling statements to me:

> *They were continually devoting themselves to the apostles' teaching and to fellowship, to the breaking of bread and to prayer. Everyone kept feeling a sense of awe; and many wonders and signs were taking place through the apostles. And all those who had believed were together and had all things in common; and they began selling their property and possessions and were sharing them with all, as anyone might have need. Day by day continuing with one mind in the temple and breaking bread from house to house, they were taking their meals together with gladness and sincerity of heart, praising God and having favor with all the people and the Lord was adding to their number day by day those who were being saved (Acts 2:42-47).*

> *And when they had prayed, the place where they had gathered together was shaken, and they were all filled with the Holy Spirit and began to speak the word of God with boldness. And the congregation of those who believed were of one heart and soul; and not one of them claimed that anything belonging to him was his own, but all things were common property to them. And with great power the apostles were giving testimony to the resurrection of the Lord Jesus, and abundant grace was upon them all. For there was not a needy person among them, for all who were owners of land or houses would sell them and bring the proceeds of the sales and lay them at*

the apostles' feet, and they would be distributed to each as any
had need (Acts 4:31-35).

At the hands of the apostles many signs and wonders were
taking place among the people; and they were all with one
accord in Solomon's portico. But none of the rest dared to
associate with them; however, the people held them in high
esteem. And all the more believers in the Lord, multitudes
of men and women, were constantly added to their number,
to such an extent that they even carried the sick out into the
streets and laid them on cots and pallets, so that when Peter
came by at least his shadow might fall on any one of them.
Also the people from the cities in the vicinity of Jerusalem
were coming together, bringing people who were sick or af-
flicted with unclean spirits, and they were all being healed
(Acts 5:12-16).

The early believers were all of one mind, one accord and
were all filled with the Holy Spirit. All their needs were being met and great signs and wonders were taking place. How
did all this happen? Why don't we see these things prevalent
among us today?

I think Acts 2:37 may give us some insight, *"Now when they*
heard this, they were pierced to the heart, and said to Peter and the
rest of the apostles, 'Brethren, what shall we do?'"

After being told they had crucified the Christ, they were all
pierced, their hearts were wounded and they cried out to know
what to do. It happened to all 3000 of them, so they truly were
of one heart and simply maintained that rhythm. This heart
piercing, this *sacred wound* to the heart is much like the man
with the broken back; it does not require much of a touch to get
a response from a heart like this.

While I was working on this chapter I saw a picture in my
mind's eye of a man with an ice pick protruding from his chest.
This man was not full of arguments or opinions but was totally
focused on the sharp metal object lodged in his heart. He simply wanted to respond to the "touch" on his heart so he could
re-establish equilibrium (a healthy rhythm) in his heart again.
Acts 2:37 says, *"They* (plural) *were pierced to the heart"* (emphasis
mine).

People whose hearts are easily touched by God are easily

in unity with Him and with each other. Spiritual distinctions are good and will always be with us, but divisions, suspicions, competition and hidden agendas must be done away with if Jesus' prayer for the church in John 17 is to be one of reality.

> *I do not ask on behalf of these alone, but for those also who believe in Me through their word; that they may all be one; even as You, Father, are in Me and I in You, that they also may be in us, so that the world may believe that You sent Me. The glory which You have given Me I have given to them, that they may be one, just as We are one; I in them and You in Me, that they may be perfected in unity, so that the world may know that You sent Me, and loved them, even as You have loved Me. Father, I desire that they also, whom You have given Me, be with Me where I am, so that they may see My glory which You have given Me, for You loved Me before the foundation of the world. O righteous Father, although the world has not known You, yet I have known You; and these have known that You sent Me; and I have made Your name known to them, and will make it known, so that the love with which You loved Me may be in them and I in them* (John 17:20-26).

A touchable heart, a heart opened by God and open to God, is essential to our oneness with the Lord and our oneness as the body of Christ. "O Lord, give us hearts that are easily touched by You and that are moved by what moves Your heart. Amen."

3

A Fascinated Heart

What fascinates you? What grabs your attention, grips your affection and gears up your imagination? We have so many issues and options that vie for our time that few of us can say that only one thing is on our radar at the moment. The plethora of choices and variety of opportunities in which we could become engaged spins our heads and confuses our hearts. We get tossed between what is real and the smoke and mirrors of the virtually real, and it dims our vision and dissipates our spiritual appetite and passions. All of this makes these words from Psalm 73 even more challenging.

Whom have I in Heaven but You? And besides You, I desire nothing on earth. My flesh and my heart may fail, but God is the strength of my heart and my portion forever. For, behold, those who are far from You will perish; you have destroyed all those who are unfaithful to You. But as for me, the nearness of God is my good; I have made the Lord God my refuge, that I may tell of all Your works (Psalm 73:25-28).

Amazing. These words were written by a human being under the Holy Spirit's influence and we know they are true, since they are in the Bible. The Psalmist says that he looks to no one else in Heaven; and he delights in nothing else on earth. Are you delighting in the Lord alone? Are you fascinated with His

heart of immeasurable grace and limitless love? Are you taken
by the breadth of its mercy, beauty and wisdom? There are so
many glorious components of His nature and His character
that capture and fascinate our hearts. Yet book after book, and
article after article come to my desk about how bored Christians are, and how they are not moved inwardly to abandon
their hearts to God. We are so in touch with the pulse of our
culture that many are sadly out of rhythm with Heaven's heart.

> *"Whom have I in heaven but you? And besides You, I desire*
> *nothing on earth. My flesh and my heart may fail, but God*
> *is the strength of my heart and my portion forever"* (Psalm
> 73:25-26).

Mike Bickle provides insight on this passage from *The Sev-
en Longings of the Human Heart.*

> Let these words settle on you. Let your heart meet
> these verses head-on. Be confronted, challenged, com-
> forted and convicted by the depth of this passage.
> Open the door of your heart and invite Him to clean
> up all the religious messes and worldly entanglements
> and freshly fascinate you with the wonder that is God's
> presence living in you. Receive the invigorating touch
> of His Spirit who longs to encounter you and has not
> changed in His heart toward you. Simply permit God
> to be Himself. Cooperate with the Holy Spirit as He
> comes to make Jesus more real to you and like the
> morning dew on the grass make even the familiar and
> new inviting (p. 42).

Don't fear, fret or back away because you have been spiritually dry or wayward in your walk with God. He is not counting on you to be dependable (Remember King David?) but He
is calling you to totally depend on Him. I love Psalm 73:26,
where Asaph wrote, *"My flesh and my heart may fail but God is
the strength of my heart and my portion forever."* He is saying that
my humanness might fail me, I might mess up, but God is the
rock-solid strength of my heart. He is mine and I am His, no
matter what.

There is no doubt in my mind that Asaph had experienced

what he wrote. He knew what it was like to desire and delight in knowing the Lord above everything else. I don't know if he lived in that place continually, but he at least had known God in that way and knew he could encounter Him again in a similar fashion. God had captured Asaph's heart and he was completely taken with the person of God. Asaph had found his delight in the magnificence of God and even if he didn't do everything just right, he knew that he was not down for the count. The Lord had captivated his heart and He was the strength and the rock of Asaph's heart. God had enabled him to sense the rhythm of His heart, and God had not altered His posture toward Asaph. The Lord empowered Asaph to delight in Him and His ways and He would help Asaph find that place and maintain that place based on His power.

This is why he says, *"But as for me, the nearness of God is my good; I have made the Lord God my refuge"* (Psalm 73:28). God's presence, His nearness, gave Asaph the encouragement and unction to trust and rely on Him and find the present-tense impetus to again desire God above all else.

Asaph knew that even when other people irked him or when their words and actions tried to disrupt the rhythm of his heart he could keep his heart attuned with God. *"Great peace have they which love Thy law and nothing shall offend them"* (Psalm 119:165, KJV).

The flow of life between Asaph's heart and God's did not have to suffer worldly interruption. Here we learn that the heart of an individual who truly loves God and His Word is filled with peace and does not have to be filled with resentment. A heart that remains captured does not have to be blocked by the *sludge of a grudge* and does not have to break rhythm. There is a peace that transcends reason and flows in the rhythm of a heart that has been captured by God.

David, this man who we know had a God-ward heart, gives us some insight here:

One thing I have asked from the Lord, that I shall seek: that I may dwell in the house of the Lord all the days of my life, to behold the beauty of the Lord and to meditate in His temple. For in the day of trouble He will conceal me in His tabernacle; in the secret place of His tent He will hide me; He will lift

*me up on a rock. And now my head will be lifted up above my
enemies around me, and I will offer His tent sacrifices with
shouts of joy; I will sing, yes I will sing, praises to the Lord.
Hear, O Lord, when I cry with my voice and be gracious to
me and answer me. When you said, 'Seek My face,' my heart
said to You, 'Your face, O Lord, I shall seek'* (Psalm 27:4-8).

David tips us off to a vital principle. He asks God for *one
thing,* to perpetually live in God's presence so He can behold
His beauty, or literally the *delightfulness* of God. David had beheld the incomprehensible beauty and delightful perfection of
God's character and nature and he was spoiled for anything
and everything else. He simply wanted to experience the tran-
scendent magnificence of the Lord and spend his time medi-
tating on and recapturing this to the delight of his own heart.
When he could do this, he certainly had no trouble trusting
God to protect him, fight for him or provide for him. It was no
effort for David, in light of glimpsing how delightful God is, to
seek His face and follow hard after Him in obedience.

One other little insight we can get from David is the God-
side of the equation. We find this in Psalm 18:19, *"He brought me
forth also into a broad place; He rescued me, because He delighted in
me."* When David beheld the beauty and delightfulness of God,
and meditated before Him about what he had seen, in his heart
he found out something that astounded him. Not only did David delight in God; God showed David that He delighted in
him! No doubt this truth added to the wonder and passion that
David had for the Lord. How could this indefinably glorious
God of all that is find delight in this incredibly human individual known as David? But He did, and the best news is that
He really does delight in us too. He delights in us and in His
plans for us. He delights in our love for Him in and our prayers
to Him. Part of the beauty of God is to delight in people who
are not thoroughly delightful. This truth adds strength and stability to our hearts and gives us fresh reasons to be fascinated
with Him and by Him.

Listen. You can almost hear God's Spirit lift the words of
James 4:8 off the page and deposit them in your heart, *"Draw
near to Me and I will draw near to you...."* He woos us to pursue
Him and when we do, He draws close to us. He wants us to

comprehend the purpose for which He apprehended us. *Relationship. Intimacy.* He wants us to abide in Him, and to experience Him abiding in us. The things of earth certainly grow dim as we bask in the light of His countenance. Fascinating - absolutely fascinating. His love exceeds our description, His power transcends our vocabulary. His wonderful offer of a life with Him simply awaits our acceptance.

4

A Heart that Is Given to God

One Sunday morning as the worship team was walking out of the prayer room, I shared the main verse I was going to preach on that day with my executive pastor, Doug Day. The verse was Proverbs 23:26, *"Give me your heart, my son, and let your eyes delight in My ways."*

Doug related this true story to me and I always refer to it when I speak on this topic. Doug was the cross country team manager for a local college and went to all the meets. The athletes were running on a cold blustery day on a course filled with steep hills. The cross country coach stood at the top of the hill near the finish line, and as each runner approached the bottom of the last hill he yelled to them by name, "Bill, give me your heart; give me your heart; I want your heart! Steve, give me your heart; give me your heart; I want your heart!" He gave this exhortation to each runner as he pushed toward the finish line. Why did he do this? Was it so he could be known as the most inspiring coach? No. He simply wanted the best from his men. He wanted them to finish and he wanted their best. He wanted them to win and he knew that in order to do so they could hold nothing back. They had to give their all. They had to give their heart away; nothing else and nothing less would suffice.

I believe that the Lord calls out to us, "My son, give me

your heart," because He wants His best for us, and His best for us comes via a surrendered heart. He doesn't say, "Give me your time, your talent, or give me your money," though He will get those if He gets your heart! He most certainly does not say, "Give me your opinion." He wants what is best for us so He does say, "Give me your heart." This is both an invitation and a command. You don't have to release your heart to Him, but He wants you to and He wants you *to want* to do it. It's a command in that the Lord equates obedience with love, and He wants us to love Him because loving Him is what is the highest and best for us (John 14:21).

A heart that is freely given to God comes more easily into rhythm with His heart. He captures our hearts so we can freely give them away and then give our hearts back to Him, that we might be fully captured by Him. He tells us to give Him our hearts because if we don't, we'll give our hearts to something or someone else and we will end up broken, fallen and confused. He wants your heart because He wants you to win the prize of a life fulfilled in Him. He wants your heart because He doesn't want you to lose your honor, your dignity, your integrity, your future, your value or your purpose in the Kingdom. The desire of the Father's heart is, "Give me your heart."

There is another truly endearing aspect to the truth we find in this proverb. The second part of the verse helps us see further into God's call for us to give Him our hearts. Proverbs 23:26: *"Give me your heart, my son, and let your eyes delight in My ways."* He wants our hearts so we are freer to let, allow, permit and direct our eyes to delight in God's ways. There is a true cause and effect relationship here. If we give our hearts to Him then we can more freely and fully discern God's ways and find our delight in them.

Where do you find your delight? What is your heart given to? There is a definite correlation to the depth and definition of what you delight in and the rhythm of your heart. Your eyes are bound to delight in something, and your heart is the directional indicator. God wants to reveal His delightfulness to us (See David in chapter 3) but we must get our heart in synch with Him so we will be alert to His delightful ways.

Moses helps us see this truth in his relationship with the Lord. In Psalm 103:7 we read these words, *"He made known His ways to Moses, His acts to the sons of Israel."*

The people of Israel knew all about the miraculous things that God did for them. But they did not have the personal connection and intimacy with God that He longed for, and that which they truly needed. Moses was different because he knew who God *was*, not just the things God *did*. We see this displayed in Exodus 33:12-17:

> *Then Moses said to the Lord, "See, You say to me, 'Bring up this people!' But You Yourself have not let me know whom You will send with me. Moreover, You have said, 'I have known you by name, and you have also found favor in My sight.' Now therefore, I pray You, if I have found favor in Your sight, let me know Your ways that I may know You, so that I may find favor in Your sight. Consider too, that this nation is Your people." And He said, "My presence shall go with you, and I will give you rest." Then he said to Him, "If Your presence does not go with us, do not lead us up from here. For how then can it be known that I have found favor in Your sight, I and Your people? Is it by Your going with us, so that we, I and Your people, may be distinguished from all the other people who are upon the face of the earth?" The Lord said to Moses, "I will also do this thing of which you have spoken; for you have found favor in My sight and I have know you by name."*

Moses had given his heart to God, and now he truly desired to know His ways so he could more completely know God. I love this verse, and I challenge you to make this the cry of your heart.

"O God, that I might know Your ways that I might know You that I might find favor in Your sight." This is remarkable ammunition for your prayer gun!

You will find God's heart wide open to you. He is ready to train your eyes to delight in His ways so you can more deeply love Him and be loved by Him. This will empower you to know His immeasurable goodness in ways you previously could not even imagine.

The next level of Moses' relationship with God was at hand. God was drawing Moses unto Himself to experience a place where God would reveal His glory to him in an unprecedented encounter. God prompted Moses to release his heart to Him in a fresh way because He in turn wanted to reveal Himself in a whole new dimension to Moses.

> *The Lord said to Moses, "I will also do this thing of which you have spoken; for you have found favor in My sight and I have known you by name." Then Moses said, "I pray You, show me Your glory!" And He said, "I Myself will make all My goodness pass before you, and will proclaim the name of the Lord before you; and I will be gracious to whom I will be gracious, and will show compassion on whom I will show compassion." But He said, "You cannot see My face, for no man can see Me and live!" Then the Lord said, "Behold, there is a place by Me, and you shall stand there on the rock; and it will come about, while My glory is passing by, that I will put you in the cleft of the rock and cover you with My hand until I have passed by. Then I will take My hand away and you shall see My back, but My face shall not be seen"* (Exodus 33:17-23).

> *The Lord descended in the cloud and stood there with him…. Then the Lord passed by in front of him and proclaimed, "The Lord, the Lord God, compassionate and gracious, slow to anger, and abounding in loving kindness and truth; who keeps loving kindness for thousands, who forgives iniquity, transgression and sin…." Moses made haste to bow low toward the earth and worship* (Exodus 34:5-8).

God wanted Moses to know the inner workings of His heart. The Lord revealed how compassionate, gracious and slow to anger He is. The Father unveiled how full of loving kindness, truth and forgiveness He truly is. He wanted Moses' eyes trained to see Him in these ways so Moses' heart could be full of how delightful God is. He wants that for you too, "My son, give Me your heart," this is God's heart for us.

Surely a captured heart is a heart fully given to God and trained to delight in His ways.

5

Upward and Inward

I was praying and journaling, as is my practice, and one day I heard these words rumble forth, "The upward quest and the inward connection." The Lord was sharing with me two vital elements that help establish the rhythm of our hearts. The upward quest and the inward connection; both of these are essential and both merit our attention.

Paul stated in Colossians 3:1-5:

> *Therefore if you have been raised up with Christ, keep seeking the things above, where Christ is, seated at the right hand of God. Set your mind on the things above, not on the things that are on earth. For you have died and your life is hidden with Christ in God. When Christ, who is our life, is revealed, then you also will be revealed with Him in glory. Therefore consider the members of your earthly body as dead to immorality, impurity, passion, evil desire, and greed, which amounts to idolatry.*

We are instructed to seek the things above and to set our minds on things that are above, not on things that are on the earth. These are things that we must choose to do. God does not just zap us and instantaneously cause this upward focus to become an ever-present reality to us. The upward quest requires our pressing on and pressing in to God's heart.

Paul gives us this insight in Philippians 3:13-14, *"Brethren, I do not regard myself as having laid hold of it yet; but one thing I do: forgetting what lies behind and reaching forward to what lies ahead, I press on toward the goal for the prize of the upward call of God in Christ Jesus."*

Paul describes himself as reaching forward and pressing toward this goal. It is this upward quest that empowers him to forget what lies behind, both successes and failures, and to carry on. It is this vertical pursuit that energizes him to consider himself dead to things like immorality, impurity, evil desire and the other earthly pulls on his life. This frees him to seek the things that are above and beyond his present level of experience and compels him to lock-in his thoughts and affections on the heart of Heaven.

Paul's heart is intent on "running to win" (1 Corinthians 9:24) and "pressing on to maturity," (Hebrews 6:1). God gives power to the pursuit (2 Corinthians 5:17) and this pursuit releases power to us as we gain new levels of the incredible value of *knowing Him* and the power of His resurrected life (Philippians 3:8-10). This is much like the thrust of a missile that breaks gravity's hold on it as it flies heaven-ward. A power greater than earth's gravitational pull is exerted by the missile and is released to access its target. A heart that is filled with the Word and with the Spirit is thrust upward and locked onto its target, the heart of God.

Have you ever prayed about going to a new level in your relationship with God? Has anyone ever prayed that for you? The Bible tells us that there are no limits to His Lordship and that the increase of His kingdom or government is endless (Isaiah 9:7).

One key to going onward in God is growing upward in our relationship with Him. We must relate to Him where He is and as He is. He is seated in heavenly places on the throne of all authority and power, and we must pursue Him in this fashion. God draws us to this upward quest to free our hearts from weights and the sins that so easily cause us to stumble. This vertical connection, this upward quest fixes our focus on Him and causes us to be more aware of His presence and fortifies us to walk blameless before Him. This upward quest is part of what establishes the rhythm of our heart.

The Lord is on His throne in the heavenlies, but He also

lives in the heart of every believer. We learn in Romans 8:9 that we are in the Spirit because the Spirit of God dwells in us. I have always loved 1 Corinthians 6:17, *"But the one who joins himself to the Lord is one spirit with Him."* We are intricately and inseparably joined together, my human spirit with the Spirit of God. WOW! We must come to know the Spirit of God who lives within us on an intimate level. The Holy Spirit joined to my spirit is the *inward connection* that I journaled about. How do we grow deeper in our knowledge of Him? How do we get our own hearts synchronized with Him?

I've lived by a rule that has served me well for many years. My response in most difficult or demanding situations was to simply *go low*. I found that if I were willing to go low, to humble myself before God and man, that God's grace would give me all I required to accomplish what I needed in each scenario that I faced. This is still good advice, but a few years ago the Lord brought about a new twist to my trusted method of operation. He instructed me that going low was good and that it had been pleasing to Him, beneficial to others and an instrument of growth for me.

Then He opened up a new perspective to me. I heard these words in my heart, "John, I don't just want you to go low, I want you to go deep." He referenced Psalm 42:7, *"Deep calls to deep...."* He wanted to speak to a different place in me. He wanted me to understand the depth of His heart more accurately, and to do this I had to go deeper in Him. I understood that this exhortation was for me to connect with the Spirit of God within me in a more mature fashion. A new adventure was beginning and I was going to discover *deep* as I had not yet known it.

I pondered this call to deep and my cry instantly turned to Ephesians 3:14-21:

> *For this reason I bow my knees before the Father, from whom every family in heaven and on earth derives its name, that He would grant you, according to the riches of His glory, to be strengthened with power through His Spirit in the inner man, so that Christ may dwell in your hearts through faith; and that you, being rooted and grounded in love, may be able to comprehend with all the saints what is the breadth*

and length and height and depth, and to know the love of Christ which surpasses knowledge, that you may be filled up to all the fullness of God. Now to Him who is able to do far more abundantly beyond all that we ask or think, according to the power that works within us, to Him be the glory in the church and in Christ Jesus to all generations forever and ever. Amen.

It takes the love and power of God to grow in our relationship to the God who is love and who has all power. My pursuit of knowing the Spirit of God who lives within me at a deeper level produced these words in my journal: I sensed the Lord saying this to me.

Depth is where wisdom is stored. Depth is where whispers are heard and secrets are discovered. Depth is the place where efforts exerted uncover effortless levels of revelation, discovery, understanding and truth-divided...bite size truth that is core level, life-changing, discernible and applicable.

Depth is the result of abiding in Me and My word and My Spirit abiding in you.

Depth will occur if you don't inhibit or prohibit it from happening. Spiritual gravity will pull you to new depths as you abide and obey.

Deep calls to deep. My breakers are to result in breakthroughs. The breakers pummel and humble, but they also promote and catapult you to a depth you would not otherwise gain. Waves of humble pursuit result in waves of grace and wisdom. Those things that I describe as "abundantly beyond what you can ask or think" are deeper things. Those are things beyond your present level of perception and beyond what you can conceive in your mind, heart or imagination; those are the things He has on tap for you as you follow Him to the depths of knowledge.

The upward quest leads us to the very heart of the living God. The inward connection leads us to the full expression of God's very heart in us and through us toward others. May our hearts be given to this upward quest and to this inward connection.

6

Discovering the Pleasure Principle

Don't you want to live a life that pleases God? Me too! My desire has long been to please Him. I have always had a drive within me to honor, obey and glorify Him. I think most Christians feel that way. I get tremendously frustrated when my theology is so much better than my walk with God, and it was at one such point in my life that the Lord opened a little secret that helped me so much and freed me to grow in wonderful ways:

> *For you were formerly darkness, but now you are light in the Lord; walk as children of light for the fruit of the light consists in all goodness and righteousness and truth, trying to learn what is pleasing to the Lord. Do not participate in the unfruitful deeds of darkness, but instead even expose them* (Ephesians 5:8-11).

The Bible says that I can walk in the light as I am trying to learn what is pleasing to Him. Terrific! I don't have to have all my ducks in a row. I don't have to have every biblical truth actualized and fully functional in my life to be a pleasure to Him. He likes the fact that I am purposefully trying to learn what brings pleasure to His heart. Isn't it strange that Jesus came to save us because we could never be perfect, and yet we often try to require perfection of ourselves?

If you want to totally mess up the rhythm of your heart for God, try requiring perfection of all your thoughts, words and deeds. While you are at it, see how you feel when you require these things from your friends and family. You will very soon arrive at new levels of misery and despair and risk the opportunity of becoming so condemned or self-righteous that no one will want to be around you.

If you are a Christian, then you are a child of light, and you can walk in the light. The results of being *of the light* are goodness, righteousness and truth, which are all produced at varying levels as you learn to walk in a manner that pleases Him. If you think you have learned it all or that you have figured out how to please Him then you are missing the tempo of His heart for you.

1 John 5:5-10 says it like this:

> *Who is the one who overcomes the world, but he who believes that Jesus is the Son of God? This is the One who came by water and blood, Jesus Christ; not with the water only, but with the water and with the blood It is the Spirit who testifies, because the Spirit is the truth. For there are three that testify: the Spirit and the water and the blood; and the three are in agreement. If we receive the testimony of men, the testimony of God is greater; for the testimony of God is this, that He has testified concerning His Son. The one who believes in the Son of God has the testimony in himself; the one who does not believe God has made Him a liar, because he has not believed in the testimony that God has given concerning His Son.*

God is light, there is no darkness in Him, and He is in us so we can walk in the light with Him. God is truth. Truth means reality. God is the ultimate reality. If we are to be godly, then we must be real, and it is in this truthful authenticity that we relate to Him and enjoy relationship with others who love Him (1 John 1:6-7). When we walk with Him in the reality of His truth and light, we are sensitive to our short-comings and sins, we readily confess them, and are forgiven and cleansed. It pleases God when our lives bear the fruit of the light (goodness, righteousness and truth). It also pleases Him when we confess that we have sinned and experience His amazing forgiveness as He gives us a clean slate.

The Lord does not expect perfection from you and me, only our triune God is perfect. His requirement of us is to walk blameless before Him, not sinless. If we walk blamelessly before Him, we will not be sinless but we will sin less. Cool!

This truth will release your heart to go for God with a fresh abandonment. When we recognize that trying to learn how to please Him is something that pleases Him, then it brings a new impetus to grow in God. I will not reach perfection, but I will grow in my love and relationship with the One who is perfect, and then I will be made more like Him. When we delight in His perfection He is freer to form us into the image of His Son, with whom He is perfectly pleased. He pours His love in our hearts not because we have reached perfection in our walk, but because we are walking in the grace and love of the sinless Son of God.

When we walk in the light of God's indwelling presence and in the light of His perfect words, we often become more aware of how incredible God is. The other thing we are sensitized to is how acutely human we are. This can cause a real sense of consternation in our soul and upset the equilibrium of our heart. These words from Psalm 86 can be of great value if that happens to you.

> *Teach me Your way, O LORD; I will walk in Your truth; Unite my heart to fear Your name. I will give thanks to You, O Lord my God, with all my heart, and will glorify Your name forever. For Your loving kindness toward me is great, and You have delivered my soul from the depths of Sheol* (Psalm 86:11-13).

Remember that we are walking before the Lord, trying to learn what pleases Him. David tells us that we should cry out to God to teach us His way, so we can more fully walk in His truth. We need to ask God to unite our hearts (an open admission that oftentimes our hearts are divided). As God unites our hearts to more completely love Him, fear Him, and know Him, then we can give thanks to Him and worship Him with all of our hearts. So ask God to unite your heart to fear His name so you can love Him whole-heartedly in return. Jeremiah 29:13 says, *"You will seek Me and find Me when you search for Me with all your heart."*

Isn't that just like God? He draws us unto a place where He can empower our whole-heartedness so that He can bless us for pursuing Him with all of our hearts. "O God, please unite our hearts to function like Yours!"

7

An Empowered Partnership

We all recognize certain days as having critical historical significance in our lives. We think of July 4th, September 11th, December 25th and other days that remind of us of important events that have greatly influenced our existence. March 14, 1974 is a day that might not be circled on your calendar, but it certainly is a red-letter day on mine. I met the Lord Jesus on that day, and entered into a level of life that I never dreamed was possible. The Lord initiated a life partnership with me on that March day that has defined the path of my life in ways that I am still discovering.

Paul gives us a definition of what walking with God looks like in 2 Corinthians 6:1-2, *"And working together with Him, we also urge you not to receive the grace of God in vain for He says, 'At the acceptable time I listened to you, and on the day of salvation I helped you.' Behold, now is **the acceptable time,** behold, now is **the day of salvation"** (emphasis mine).

Paul shows us some simple but vital details in this passage. I love how he defines our partnership here. This statement, *"Working together with Him...."* describes our active partnership with the living God. It is the out-working of our partnership with God that causes us to receive His grace and function in His purposes for us. Christians are co-laborers or co-workers with God (1 Corinthians 3:9). We are referred to as *His workmanship,* and we have works to do in cooperation with the Holy Spirit that He planned and prepared for us before we were born or born again (Ephesians 2:10). When we partner with Him to receive His grace and be led by His Spirit, He makes this joint venture a fruitful one.

Have you ever read 2 Corinthians 6:1 in the Amplified Bible? Check this out:

> *Laboring together [as God's fellow workers] with Him then, we beg of you not to receive the grace of God in vain [that merciful kindness by which God exerts His holy influence on souls and turns them to Christ, keeping and strengthening them—do not receive it to no purpose].*

Our partnership facilitates our heart as God's fellow workers to receive His grace. What a relationship this is! We get to have the Lord's holy influence upon our lives, not exclusively for our own pleasure (though it certainly is pleasurable) but unto His divine purposes. This will make your heart race with zeal and rest in assurance all at the same time. He not only grants us His salvation and entrance to Heaven, but He has plans for a dynamic life partnership *right now*. He readily receives us and grants us His grace when we come to Him, but He wants us to understand that He gives us life so that He can release it through us in ways that He has planned. We become His partners and He intends that partnership to be full of life and purpose.

Our partnership with God is His idea. He is the senior partner and we co-operate and co-labor with Him. Awareness of this alliance and full participation as His co-laborer is what makes us fruitful and what helps keep us faithful.

The devil does not want you to understand or function in this connection with Jesus. If he cannot keep you from recognizing the reality of this union, he will certainly try to keep it from being empowered and productive. One of the enemies' chief weapons is what I call *the nullifiers*.

Satan cannot keep God from lavishing His grace on you, but if the evil one can cause that grace to be null and void (empty and without purpose or result) then he will have effectively short-circuited the partnership. How does the devil do this?

Let's start answering that question by looking at grace. What is God's grace? I like to define grace this way:

Grace is unmerited favor from God (Romans 5:1-2).

Grace is God's divine adequacy for us (2 Corinthians 12:9-10).

Grace is the desire and power to do God's will (Philippians 2:13).

I believe that we will never consistently walk by faith until we stand by grace (Romans 5:1-2). If I can't stand strong then walking is a most shaky exercise. We know that we are to walk by faith (2 Corinthians 5:7) and that without faith we cannot please God (Hebrews 11:6).

If we do not stand by grace and are severely limited in our faith walk, then we will have received God's grace in vain, and will not have lived out our empowered union with God. Do you see how the nullifying tactics can negate the effectiveness of this cooperative venture? If we do not fully comprehend God's grace then we don't fulfill His plans for the partnership.

A key element in the enemy's strategy is to keep you tethered to your humanness and to obscure the work of the cross in your life. If we overcome this terrorist subterfuge of the devil, we can totally participate in our partnership with God and revel in the results.

To do this, we have to get our hearts in full synchronization with God on this issue. We are forgiven. Jesus did it all. It is finished. He took our sin and we are totally forgiven.

Paul says it this way, *"He made Him who knew no sin to be sin on our behalf, so that we might become the righteousness of God in Him"* (2 Corinthians 5:21). Jesus took the test. He got a 100%, a perfect score, and God gives us Jesus' grade.

2 Corinthians 5:19 gives us great help to see the reality of God's heart toward us. *"It was God [personally present] in Christ, reconciling and restoring the world to favor with Himself, not counting up and holding against [men] their trespasses [but cancelling them], and committing to us the message of reconciliation [of the restoration to favor]"* (Amplified Bible).

Jesus died for our sins, and God is not counting our sins against us. He cancelled them all. Colossians 2:14 says, *"Having cancelled out the certificate of debt consisting of decrees against us, which was hostile to us; and He has taken it out of the way, having nailed it to the cross."*

We are forgiven. We are free. We don't deserve such a gift, but God is merciful and gracious. He put us in His Son and His Son within us, and we have peace with God. The emancipation proclamation has been issued—*"For he who has died is freed from sin"* (Romans 6:7). We know it but many of us don't actualize what we know; we need this in our hearts, not just our minds. He who has died (past-tense) is free (present tense) from sin.

Knowing this truth at a core level frees us to believe, receive and to function in our partnership with God. He chose you to live for Him and He sent His Spirit to live in you. Would a Holy God live in you and seat you in His Son in heavenly places, in His presence, if you were not cleansed and forgiven in His sight? We are forgiven by God. We have His unearned favor. He makes us adequate in spite of our inadequacies and He has partnered with us by placing His Spirit in us to prompt and empower us to do His will. What an amazing arrangement. What an inviting partnership!

I discovered a wonderful insight concerning this whole empowered partnership issue in Colossians 1:5-6. *"The gospel which has come to you, just as in all the world also it is constantly bearing fruit and increasing, even as it has been doing in you also since the day you heard of it and understood the grace of God in truth."*

The word for *truth* here means *reality*. The fruitfulness and increase of God's powerful work on people's lives was evidenced when they came to know the reality of God's grace. This happened when they heard and *understood* the reality of God's grace, not just when they heard about it. When they knew they were forgiven and that God loved them, delighted in them and had given them His favor, His divine adequacy and fruitfulness came. When they partnered with God's Spirit to know and walk out God's will for them, increase came. Realizing that God's grace was theirs energized a spread of the Gospel in a mighty way. They experienced His empowered partnership.

This is what He has planned for all of us. Will you re-align yourself and partner with Him today? Ask Him to nullify the attempt by the enemy to make His grace void of purpose in your life. Lock into His heart for you today and receive the joy to be His workmanship and His co-laborer in the life that His Spirit longs to release through you.

The Christian life is a partnership—a day-by-day, moment-by-moment, 24-7-365 proposition. He lives within us and He never slumbers. He is always in us, stirring us, leading us and directing us to walk out the purposes He apprehended us for. We don't have to figure it all out. We *follow* it out.

I love these words in Psalm 132:3-5, *"Surely I will not enter my house, nor lie on my bed; I will not give sleep to my eyes Or slumber to my eyelids, until I find a place for the Lord, a dwelling place for the Mighty One of Jacob."*

I believe that the Lord wants to find a dwelling place in us where He is the senior partner. He is Lord and He wants to call the shots in our lives. This is not because His is egotistical, but because He is supremely loving and kind, and wants only what is best for us. He knows that the very best life we can live is when we are firmly planted in His grace, walking by faith, empowered by His Spirit and fruitful in experience.

Partnership anyone?

8

A Runner's Heart

There is a precious principle and some valuable lessons nestled in a story about Absalom, Joab and David. You have no doubt read and heard much about David and Absalom. Many of us are also familiar with Joab's name as well, but for me the hero of this story is Ahimaaz. Ahimaaz? Who in the world is Ahimaaz? I hope that you will come to know and appreciate Ahimaaz, and learn the heart lesson that he had so beautifully mastered.

Here's a synopsis of the story told in 2 Samuel 18:5-33. David's rebellious son Absalom was warring against him, and David was forced to send his army to fight against his son. The decree of David's heart was clear, *"Deal gently for my sake with the young man Absalom"* (2 Samuel 18:5). David did not want Absalom to be harmed. He knew what was in the Father's heart toward Absalom and he wanted to leave Absalom's future to the dealings of God. It certainly appeared that Absalom would be dealt with as he had become entangled in the limbs of an oak tree and was dangling by his head.

Joab had a better idea than David, or so he thought. He was a warrior and it was his purpose to win the battle, so he put three spears in Absalom's body and turned him over to ten other soldiers who finished him off. Joab was a warrior like David, but he was not a worshipper. David was a man with a heart after God, while Joab was a man with a heart for conquest. Joab's heart left no room to respect David's love for his son or God's lordship of His chosen people. Joab's lust for victory trumped his loyalty to the king and to the King of kings.

After Absalom's death, Ahimaaz enters the picture. His first thought is to run to King David and give him the news that he had won and the rebellion was over. Joab told Ahimaaz that he had chosen another runner to carry the report to David and that Ahimaaz could take the day off. He was off the clock, he had no orders, no directive to run and there would be no compensation or outward reward for him to run to the king. Then Ahimaaz makes a statement that has gripped my heart since the day I understood it. He tells Joab in 2 Samuel 18:23, *"'But whatever happens,' he said, 'I will run.'"*

Did you catch the significance of those words? Ahimaaz reveals his heart's motivation in this impassioned declaration. Joab completely misses the impact of what Ahimaaz has said and blurts out a single syllable response, *"Run"* (2 Samuel 18:23).

I read this many years ago and was fascinated by the heart of Ahimaaz. He loved the king and when the joy of the battle's victory was announced, all he could think of was blessing David with this news. He also knew the heartbreak that King David would experience over Absalom's death, so he wanted to be there to share in that, and to minister to the king. Even if all he could offer was his presence, he wanted to be with the king at this moment. It didn't matter that today was not his time to run. He had no concern about reward or compensation. His heart was to be there with the king so that David could be touched by his presence and he could be available to the desire of the king's heart. He was in the service of the king, and while he did not have a position of command, he had a place in his heart for David, and nothing could keep him from running into the king's presence.

What a wonderful disposition of heart toward the king and what a stark contrast to the motive of Joab's heart. Joab was all about conquering the enemy for the king's army, while Ahimaaz was all about honoring the authority of the king by serving the purpose of David's heart.

A quick glance at Ahimaaz's pedigree gives us a little insight into his motives and his character. He was a son of Zadok (2 Samuel 18:19). Zadok was a special man with a family that was dedicated to serving the Lord.

> *But the Levitical priests, the sons of Zadok, who kept charge of My sanctuary when the sons of Israel went astray from Me, shall come near to Me to minister to Me; and they shall stand before Me to offer Me the fat and the blood, declares the Lord GOD. They shall enter My sanctuary; they shall come near to My table to minister to Me and keep My charge....*
> *When they go out into the outer court, into the outer court to the people, they shall put off their garments in which they have been ministering and lay them in the holy chambers; then they shall put on other garments so that they will not transmit holiness to the people with their garments. More-over, they shall teach My people the difference between the holy and the profane, and cause them to discern between the unclean and the clean* (Ezekiel 44:15-16, 19-23).

Zadok and his sons did not go astray as many of the Levitical priests did. The Levitical priests were permitted to minister to the people, but Zadok and his sons stood in God's presence to minister to Him. They were so close to God that their clothing was permeated with His powerful presence, and simply touching their garments would transmit holiness. They lived an upright and sanctified lifestyle, and were charged with teaching God's people what He deemed holy, along with what He considered to be profane.

Ahimaaz is a son of Zadok. He knew what it was like to be in God's presence and in the presence of God's anointed king. Nothing could keep him from finding his place before David. He had a heart to run into the king's presence.

As I continued reading, I recognized something thrilling that I have prayed and longed for in the following verses. Ahimaaz had the passion of a runner's heart that beat with the values of the king.

> *Now David was sitting between the two gates; and the watch-man went up to the roof of the gate by the wall, and raised his eyes and looked, and behold, a man running by himself. The watchman called and told the king. And the king said,*

"If he is by himself there is good news in his mouth." And he came nearer and nearer. Then the watchman saw another man running; and the watchman called to the gatekeeper and said, "Behold, another man running by himself." And the king said, "This one also is bringing good news." The watchman said, "I think the running of the first one is like the running of Ahimaaz the son of Zadok." And the king said, "This is a good man and comes with good news." Ahimaaz called and said to the king, "All is well." And he prostrated himself before the king with his face to the ground. And he said, "Blessed is the LORD your God, who has delivered up the men who lifted their hands against my lord the king." The king said, "Is it well with the young man Absalom?" And Ahimaaz answered, "When Joab sent the king's servant, and your servant, I saw a great tumult, but I did not know what it was." Then the king said, "Turn aside and stand here." So he turned aside and stood still. Behold, the Cushite arrived, and the Cushite said, "Let my lord the king receive good news, for the LORD has freed you this day from the hand of all those who rose up against you." Then the king said to the Cushite, "Is it well with the young man Absalom?" And the Cushite answered, "Let the enemies of my lord the king, and all who rise up against you for evil, be as that young man!" The king was deeply moved and went up to the chamber over the gate and wept (2 Samuel 18:24-32).

King David was sitting at the gate, and his watchers were looking for messengers from the battlefield. The watchmen called out that two runners were approaching, and that one man was running like Ahimaaz. Do you see it? Ahimaaz had run so often into his presence that the king's watchmen recognized his movement. I saw this and something exploded in my heart. I cried out to God, "O Lord, I want to run to You so often, so consistently that the watchers in Heaven will recognize me when I approach You. I want to come into God's presence so often that my *g-a-i-t* is recognized at the *g-a-t-e*."

Ahimaaz had a healthy heart habit of running to the king. He did not have to be rewarded, it could be good news, bad news, or no news, but God had put a heart to run in him and his response was, *"But whatever happens...I will run"* (2 Samuel 18:23).

Ahimaaz did not get to be the one who informed the king. It simply did not matter whether it was his words, his message or his revelation of truth. He ran for one reason, and that was to be with the king, to stand in the king's presence. He did arrive in David's presence first, and he had all the information that the king wanted, but another man was commissioned to be the spokesman that day. He told David that he was "not the man" and David gave him a place to stand by him. Ahimaaz stood in silence and listened while another man entered and told David of Absalom's fate. He was satisfied because he had not run for the purpose of recognition or reward. He ran out of a heart relationship with the king.

When I think of this story and the heart that Ahimaaz had for the king I think of these words: *"When You said, 'Seek My face,' my heart said to You, 'Your face, O Lord, I shall seek'"* (Psalm 27:8).

I want my heart to say, *"Your face, O Lord, I shall seek."* I want to say that it doesn't matter what battle is raging or whether circumstances are favorable or bleak; no matter what happens I will run. *I want my gait to be known and recognized at the gate.*

"O God, give me a runner's heart because it is when I run that I feel Your pleasure."

9

A Readily Adjustable Heart

The Lord is immutable. He never changes, but things around us are constantly changing. There is a constant ebb and flow to life and things change so rapidly. The world around us moves at a dizzying pace. We must maintain our spiritual stability while being flexible and adaptable to the issues and individuals that we encounter.

Many Christians struggle to establish and keep a healthy balance under such evolving circumstances. One obstacle we constantly face is being consistent in our walk. We must stay available to God and the desire of His heart while we recalibrate our lives to respond to the un-ending barrage of new information and opportunities.

How do we keep in step with the cadence of His heart in a culture that is repeatedly re-inventing itself? We must find ways to walk in league with the Holy Spirit and be a light to an increasingly secular world at the same time.

A common tendency has arisen in the church that is truly counterproductive to our cause. It wars against the great commandment (Deuteronomy 6:4-5) and the great commission (Matthew 28:18-20). What is this tendency, this religious dilemma that plagues many of God's people? Simply stated, we fear compromise and dishonoring God, so in an effort to be spiritually stable and strong, we have become religiously rigid.

Having your heart established in God is an absolute must. Letting your heart and mind become rigid and hard is an absolute disaster. I think that we can find genuine counsel and direction for these predicaments in Romans 12:9-16.

> *Let love be without hypocrisy. Abhor what is evil; cling to what is good. Be devoted to one another in brotherly love; give preference to one another in honor; not lagging behind in diligence, fervent in spirit, serving the Lord; rejoicing in hope, persevering in tribulation, devoted to prayer, contributing to the needs of the saints, practicing hospitality. Bless those who persecute you; bless and do not curse. Rejoice with those who rejoice, and weep with those who weep. Be of the same mind toward one another; do not be haughty in mind, but associate with the lowly. Do not be wise in your own estimation* (Romans 12:9-16).

Not surprisingly, Paul takes us right to the key element of having a fixed and yet flexible heart. He tells us to love God and people without hypocrisy. Love is the real deal. Love drives fear out and it is fear, not faith, that makes our hearts grow rigid. A loveless heart is a fearful heart and a fearful heart won't please God, because fear and faith do not fruitfully coexist. We must learn from the Holy Spirit to simultaneously love what God loves and hate what He hates.

If we hold on to what is good and abhor what is evil, then we will maintain our union with God's indwelling Spirit and live out our faith with integrity before the world. This will enable us to hate evil and love evil-doers simultaneously. A rigid heart is apt to be closed and fearful, which makes it very difficult to separate the things we detest from those who are entrenched in that style of living.

Here are two ultra-basic principles to help us:

Lost people *act* like lost people. They are supposed to. They have little choice in the matter. Shame on us if we are surprised or befuddled by this fact.

The devil cheats. The devil always hides behind people and he loves it when Christians treat those people like we should be treating him.

If we are to live without being hypocrites we must know how to cast off evil and hang on to what is good. This is the mark of a heart that is in tune with the Father's heart.

Take a look at how the Amplified Bible renders Romans 12:16: *"Live in harmony with one another; do not be haughty [snobbish, high-minded, exclusive], but readily adjust yourself to [people, things] and give yourselves to humble tasks. Never overestimate yourself or be wise in your own conceits."*

I think the truth Paul portrayed here will help us have a right response to all the exhortations we find in Romans 12:9-15. We are encouraged to readily adjust ourselves to people and things. This means that in cooperation with the Holy Spirit, we can be flexible and adjustable without sin and without compromise. We can readily adjust to the cultural difference that we encounter in our everyday life. God is no respecter of persons. He loves people from every nation, tribe and tongue. He loves people whether they are young, old, male or female. He loves people with long hair, short hair, no hair, purple hair, braided hair, or in spite of their hair. We can readily adjust to each situation that we face because of the unchanging love of the One who lives within us.

We can also readily adjust to the different styles of worship that we see in the church. We must learn to respect the distinctions and directions that various churches and ministries hold as sacred. So much of what we fail to be flexible toward is not substantial; it is simply style and preference. We must know that style is not substance, activity is not anointing, personality is not power, and volume is not vitality. Most of what we get rigid about is not doctrinal heresy; it is just delivery style and church culture. All styles can be filled with God's presence and power, but none of them is just because they embody or eliminate certain trends, practices or traditions. Larry Norman's song from the 1970's, *"Why Does the Devil Have All the Good Music?"* addresses this.

Jesus wants our hearts to beat with a readily adjustable rhythm. He knows that we must function in this manner so He has placed His Spirit in our hearts to make this possible. He desires us to be fixed and flexible of heart, so He has put that kind of heart in us. It is our responsibility to discover and develop this faithful adaptability in our inner man.

The Lord wants us readily adjustable for the Father's pleasure. Look at Jesus' words in John 8:29, *"And He who sent Me is with Me; He has not left Me alone, for I always do the things that are pleasing to Him."*

Jesus knew that God had sent Him into the world and He knew that the Holy Spirit was with Him to help Him. In light of these truths, Jesus always did the things that were pleasing to the Father. Did Jesus always do the same thing in every situation? Did He always preach the same words, heal the same way, respond with the same actions or use the same methods? No, He was readily adjustable to hear what pleased God in each instance and to do accordingly. We can be led by the Holy Spirit to have a similar response if our hearts are sensitive and flexible. Our highest honor is to bring pleasure to the Father. He gives us the capacity to honor Him in this way when our hearts are subject to His bidding.

Let's review Romans 12:9-16 through the lens of the flexible heart. A heart that is flexible and easily adapted to varying circumstances is a necessity in order to live out these truths. Thank God that He has made this kind of heart available to us. Look at these instructions:

Abhor what's evil (v. 9).
Cling to what is good (v. 9).
Be devoted in brotherly love (v. 10).
Give preference to one another (v. 10).
Be diligent, fervent in spirit and service (v. 11).
Rejoice, persevere, pray (v. 12).
Give to the needy, be hospitable (v. 13).
Bless those who persecute you (v. 14).
Rejoice and weep with those who rejoice and weep (v. 15).
Be of the same mind with one another (v. 16).
Don't be wise in your own estimation (v. 16).

How are we going to be able to do all these different things with people in the varied situations that occur in our lives? We will only be able to please Him in doing all these things if we have a heart that He can easily and consistently lead and direct. For example, look at verse 10 where we read, *"Give preference to one another in honor."* The margin of the New American Standard Bible says it this way: *"Outdo one another in showing honor."*

What if I don't feel like doing that, and what if I don't think that the other people involved deserve honorable treatment? This is where you can bring your attitudes and opinions under the lordship of Jesus and into compliance with His Word. For example: we find principles like taking the last seat in Luke 14:7-11, the general call to humility and acknowledgment of our own 'stumblings' in James 3:2, and the wonderful truth that mercy triumphs over judgment in James 2:13, and we all can benefit from the reminder that love covers a multitude of sins as we read in Proverbs 10:12. He loves it when we do this, and we will love the outcome in our own lives and in the lives of others.

The heart that walks together with Him and pleases Him is a readily adjustable heart. "O God, develop that heart in me!"

10

Understanding Capacity and Proclivity

I was journaling one morning and I heard from Heaven in my heart. I had been praying about my personal limitations and failures when the Lord gave me some directions that have proved to be invaluable. These words have helped me keep my heart connected to Him in a healthy way.

I wrote this entry in my journal:

"We must not be hindered by or discouraged by our *present capacity* to walk out the Christian life because we still must be awakened and made aware of our *Spirit-given proclivity* to do so."

Capacity means our ability, aptitude or qualifications to do a certain task or work. *Proclivity* means your natural tendency or inclination toward something. This statement is packed with meaning and loaded with encouragement. God does not rely on our natural abilities or aptitudes but rather, He births new ones in us by putting His Spirit in us. When we give our hearts to Jesus Christ we become partakers of His divine nature (Hebrews 3:14, 2 Peter 1:4). This new nature has new *natural* tendencies and inclinations. Let's investigate what this means to us. (An inside tip - never measure the power of God's will by your lack of power to walk in it today.)

Paul's life story demonstrates the reality of the words that I wrote that morning. *"Circumcised the eighth day, of the nation of*

Israel, of the tribe of Benjamin, a Hebrew of Hebrews; as to the Law, a Pharisee; as to zeal, a persecutor of the church; as to the righteousness which is in the Law, found blameless" (Philippians 3:5-6).

Paul (called Saul at this time) was an enemy of the church and a zealous persecutor of Christians. *"When they had driven him out of the city, they began stoning him (Stephen); and the witnesses laid aside their robes at the feet of a young man named Saul"* (Acts 7:58).

"Saul was in hearty agreement with putting him to death..." (Acts 8:1). He participated in Stephen's stoning and was recklessly pursuing Christians. Paul was wrecking households and breaking up families with his misguided fervor for the traditions of his ancestors. His immense religious knowledge and commitment to the principles that he believed drove him to vigorously defend his faith. His abandonment to the cause was admirable, but he was dead wrong.

He was about to have a powerful confrontation with Jesus that would radically alter his life. He was about to find out how limited his capacity to really know the true God actually was. This episode would release new leanings and yearnings in him that would change the rest of his life and change the course of religious history.

As he was traveling, it happened that he was approaching Damascus, and suddenly a light from heaven flashed around him; and he fell to the ground and heard a voice saying to him, "Saul, Saul, why are you persecuting Me?" And he said, "Who are You, Lord?" And He said, "I am Jesus whom you are persecuting, but get up and enter the city, and it will be told you what you must do." The men who traveled with him stood speechless, hearing the voice but seeing no one. Saul got up from the ground, and though his eyes were open, he could see nothing; and leading him by the hand, they brought him into Damascus. And he was three days without sight, and neither ate nor drank.... But the Lord said to him (Ananias), "Go, for he is a chosen instrument of Mine, to bear My name before the Gentiles and kings and the sons of Israel; for I will show him how much he must suffer for My name's sake." So Ananias departed and entered the house, and after laying his hands on him said, "Brother Saul, the

Lord Jesus, who appeared to you on the road by which you
were coming, has sent me so that you may regain your sight
and be filled with the Holy Spirit." And immediately there
fell from his eyes something like scales, and he regained his
sight, and he got up and was baptized; and he took food and
was strengthened (Acts 9:3-9, 15-19).

Paul got saved. Paul got *radically* saved. He met the resurrected Jesus and received a new heart filled with God's Spirit.
He had a new understanding of truth and became aware of
new inclinations and tendencies that propelled his new life.

For I would have you know, brethren, that the gospel which
was preached by me is not according to man. For I neither
received it from man, nor was I taught it, but I received it
through a revelation of Jesus Christ. For you have heard of
my former manner of life in Judaism, how I used to persecute
the church of God beyond measure and tried to destroy it;
and I was advancing in Judaism beyond many of my con-
temporaries among my countrymen, being more extremely
zealous for my ancestral traditions. But when God, who
had set me apart even from my mother's womb and called
me through His grace, was pleased to reveal His Son in me
so that I might preach Him among the Gentiles, I did not
immediately consult with flesh and blood, nor did I go up
to Jerusalem to those who were apostles before me; but I
went away to Arabia, and returned once more to Damascus
(Galatians 1:11-17).

Here is a man who was skyrocketing to prominence and
recognition in his circle of influence. He was advanced in Judaism beyond many his age. Paul had charted a life course and
was going for it with gusto, until God interrupted with His
divine purpose. Paul found out that the Lord had chosen him
before he was born and that God had called Paul unto Himself.
Jesus revealed Himself to Paul's heart and that released a proclivity to know God and love Him beyond anything Paul had
ever known. Paul had been driven by zeal but he had never
been filled and led by God's Spirit, and there was simply no
comparison.

No man-made system could prompt Paul to live the life he lived once he met Jesus. Paul knew the traditions of the law, but once he met Jesus in person he began to know Him accurately and intimately. He also began to discover who he was, along with the new desire and longings that God had released into his heart. How did this happen? God made it happen.

Paul was able to say after his conversion experience, *"By the grace of God I am what I am..."* (1 Corinthians 15:10). He didn't describe himself as "not who I used to be," but by virtue of God's grace he described himself as who he was in the moment. Don't let what you have done or what you haven't done define you. Recognize that because of God's call of your life unto Him and the gift of His Spirit and His Word, you have not yet reached full capacity. Don't give up. Go on. Find out who you really are.

> *How great is the love the Father has lavished on us, that we should be called children of God! And that is what we are! The reason the world does not know us is that it did not know Him. Dear friends, now we are children of God, and what we will be has not yet been made known. But we know that when He appears, we shall be like Him, for we shall see Him as He is* (1 John 3:1-2).

We are children of God and the final outcome of our growth, maturity and fruitfulness has not been realized. We need to go on a treasure hunt. 2 Corinthians 4:7 says, *"But we have this treasure in jars of clay to show that this all-surpassing power is from God and not from us."*

We have not plumbed the depths of the treasure of life that resides within us via God's Spirit in our hearts. Don't be deceived. Many get frustrated at their present-tense capacity to walk out this life and try to salve their anxieties with pleasure. We need to pursue treasure, not just pleasure. A treasure hunt will lead you to spiritual riches and a pleasure hunt will only land you in the ditch of human discouragement. A treasure hunt will bring to us the surpassing greatness of God's power, while a pleasure hunt will only give us the best we can conceive and leave us lusting for more.

For Christ's love compels us, because we are convinced that one died for all, and therefore all died. And He died for all, that those who live should no longer live for themselves but for Him who died for them and was raised again. So from now on we regard no one from a worldly point of view. Though we once regarded Christ in this way, we do so no longer. Therefore, if anyone is in Christ, he is a new creation; the old has gone, the new has come! All this is from God, who reconciled us to Himself through Christ and gave us the ministry of reconciliation (2 Corinthians 5:14-18).

We need to get on the *new creation* band wagon. We are new creations, new creatures in Christ Jesus. We can truthfully say that the old things have passed away! We can truthfully declare that new things have come! We have a new nature with new desires and new leanings, tendencies and inclinations. Paul did not let the weight of his *natural life*, with all its wrong tendencies and inclinations, determine his destiny. The revelation of Jesus in him gave him new desires and leanings that over-powered all the *natural-ness* of his past. Amen!

We must never measure His purposes by our desire, and never measure His abilities by our weaknesses. There is within us a new Spirit-given capacity to love and obey God and, by His grace, a new proclivity to hear Him and walk with Him. "O God, awaken us to the new capacities and proclivities you have placed in us by the working of your Spirit in our lives!"

11

A Fervent Heart: Stoked and Stretched

A heart that follows hard after God's heart is one that is filled with fervency. Fervency is a normal disposition for a heart that is in love. Passivity is not normally among the descriptions of a lover's heart. My thesaurus suggests the following words for passivity—inert, inactive, unreceptive, submissive, reflexive, tameness and compliance. When was the last time you saw a love story featuring any of those words? Not likely. We need a fervent heart beating within us to fully comply with His wishes for us. God has given each believer a new heart, and He has graciously poured His love into our hearts through the Holy Spirit (Romans 5:5).

Apollos is a man we can learn from when it comes to this issue of a fervent heart.

> *Now a Jew named Apollos, an Alexandrian by birth, an eloquent man, came to Ephesus; and he was mighty in the Scriptures. This man had been instructed in the way of the Lord; and being fervent in spirit, he was speaking and teaching accurately the things concerning Jesus, being acquainted only with the baptism of John; and he began to speak out boldly in the synagogue. But when Priscilla and Aquila heard him, they took him aside and explained to him the way of God more accurately. And when he wanted to go across to Achaia, the brethren encouraged him and wrote to*

the disciples to welcome him; and when he had arrived, he
greatly helped those who had believed through grace, for he
powerfully refuted the Jews in public, demonstrating by the
Scriptures that Jesus was the Christ (Acts 18:24-28).

There are several clues to being fervent in heart in these
verses. The Word tells us that Apollos was mighty in the scriptures. We must have a current and consistent life in the Word
to keep ourselves filled with God's life and light. Apollos could
strongly declare the scriptures because he had the Word powerfully taught to him by God's Spirit. The Spirit of God revealing the Word of God to the people of God is part of the purpose
of God. Always be certain to open your Bible before the Lord
so that He can open His Word to you.

Apollos knew the word of God, but he also knew the way
of the Lord. God's ways are the personal, intimate fashion that
He has in relating to us individually. He shows us things about
His character and nature that will be most meaningful to us,
and most beneficial to those we have opportunity to minister
to in our day to day lives.

Apollos knew God's Word in a powerful manner and the
way of God in a personal fashion. These two keys helped make
him a man of true godly passion and desire and caused him to
be described as a man *fervent in spirit*. The word *fervent* means
hot-boiling, bubbling or in my terms *percolating*. This man per-
colated with spiritual fervor which no doubt had a profound
impact on those around him. It is important to note that fervent
means *boiling*, not boisterous. Fervency is measured in passion
for God, zeal for His purposes and compassion for His people, not in being loud or outgoing. My wife often reminds me,
"John, God loves introverts too." Fervency is a fiery heart, not
just a gregarious personality.

There is a hidden ingredient to fervency in these verses that
can easily be overlooked. We see in Acts 18:25-26 that Apollos
had incomplete information about the full ministry of Jesus.

Priscilla and Aquilla (who did not have all the accolades
spoken of Apollos ascribed to them) pulled him aside and
taught him. They gave him a more complete and accurate ac-
count of Jesus' life and ministry and he received it.

I propose that a fervent heart must also be a teachable

heart. All the fiery passion in Heaven will not mature you and ripen the fruit of your life if you cannot be instructed and corrected. Apollos was a man who was powerfully persuasive and wonderfully teachable. That, my friend, is the result of a true, fervent heart.

I think that this portrayal of fervency is also aptly shown in Romans chapter 12. I call this chapter "the handbook for servanthood." We see in Romans 12:11 this exhortation: *"Not lagging behind in diligence, fervent in spirit, serving the Lord...."* You may not automatically associate fervency with servanthood, but the Lord does.

If you are diligent and persistent in serving God and God's people, then you had better be percolating. Serving God is wonderful work, but it is just that: work. God's people are amazing, but we are also human and often times prove to be amazingly human. Loving God and showing compassion for people takes a heart set on fire. Showing honor to people, giving deference and preference to others, and maintaining an attitude of kindness, humility and grace requires the fire of God to be actively burning in your inner being. I like to say it like this: "A fiery fervent spirit is the forge where a servant's heart is formed." A fervent heart is a servant's heart.

A fervent heart is one that boils, bubbles and percolates with the life of God. It is a fiery heart that is teachable and knows how to serve. The fervent heart is all these things but it is something more too. Peter gives us a further insight into the outflow of a fervent heart. *"Above all, stay fervent in your love for one another, because love covers a multitude of sins"* (1 Peter 4:8).

Peter tells us that we need to be fervent in our love for one another because it is central to how we deal with our sins, as well as the sins of others among us and against us. The word here for *fervent* means something different than boiling-hot. It means "stretched out" or "to extend." It is this stretched out kind of fervent love that covers a multitude of sins.

I have a suggestion to make at this point. We know that one definition of sin means to "miss the mark." I think that a fervent, stretched-out heart of love covers others when they miss the mark. I think we need a love with *stretch-marks* that extend far enough to reach others when they miss the mark, and maybe even help cover some of the marks they made when they missed.

"Hatred stirs up strife, but love covers all transgressions" (Proverbs 10:12). Love doesn't cover-up, but it does cover. I like to say that "fervent love hovers over us and covers us until we can recover from the effects of our own sins and the sins of others against us." *"Since you have in obedience to the truth purified your souls for a sincere love of the brethren, fervently love one another from the heart"* (1 Peter 1:22).

If we are to fervently love from the heart, then we will show some spiritual stretch marks. Normal or natural human love is not refined enough and not expandable enough to consistently cover others when they sin. The fervent love God places in us can do that.

I have not been able to verify this next statement, but I have been told that it is true. When one ounce of gold has been thoroughly refined (99.99% pure) it can be stretched into a fine, thin chain that is 50 miles long. The degree of purity determines the flexibility and elasticity of the gold.

Could it be that a heart that is fervently on fire produces a heart of stretched-out love? The more a fervent heart burns in us, the more the love of God can be extended through us to others. "O Lord, may we be fervency stoked within and our love be stretched out to others."

12

A Re-Encouraged Heart

Discouragement is a common pitfall of the human heart. The spirit of this age does nothing to build you up or motivate your heart to godliness, and it does everything to bring you down and bum you out. Keeping your heart encouraged in a world system that is filled with materialism, humanism and hedonism is no small task. There is a negative downward pull that is exerted by this world, and it is all too easy to get slowed down and even sucked in.

> *Do not love the world nor the things in the world. If anyone loves the world, the love of the Father is not in him. For all that is in the world, the lust of the flesh and the lust of the eyes and the boastful pride of life, is not from the Father, but is from the world. The world is passing away, and also its lusts; but the one who does the will of God lives forever* (1 John 2:15-17).

This world system is passing away. It is dying every day and it wants to take us with it. Add to this atmospheric atrophy that we live among human disappointment, and the outworking of sin in us and through others and we realize that we are in a fight to stay encouraged. Thank God that He has sent His Spirit as our helper and some excellent instructions in His Word to empower us.

If we think that we will never face discouragement because we are Christians, then we are in for a rude awakening. If we did not get discouraged, the Lord wouldn't have included these scriptures:

> *"Wait for the LORD; be strong and let your heart take courage; yes, wait for the LORD"* (Psalm 27:14).

> *"These things I have spoken to you, so that in Me you may have peace. In the world you have tribulation, but* take *courage; I have overcome the world"* (John 16:33, my emphasis).

> *"Now may the God who gives perseverance and encouragement grant you to be of the same mind with one another according to Christ Jesus"* (Romans 15:5).

> *"Therefore encourage one another and build up one another, just as you also are doing"* (1 Thessalonians 5:11).

Several sources and means of encouragement are given to us in these scriptures. Psalm 27:14 tells us to wait for the Lord, and that our hearts can take courage as we do so. There is great encouragement for us in God's presence, and we must take advantage of being with Him. We are told for our heart to take courage as we wait before Him. He gives us encouragement when we seek His face and wait in His presence, but we must take it and appropriate it to our heart.

Jesus tells us in John 16:33 that we can take courage in His mastery of the world and His Lordship of our individual situations. Jesus has overcome this world system and *"Greater is He that is with us than he that is in the world"* (1 John 4:4). Jesus conquered the ruler of this world system and put His Spirit, who is greater, in us. This is a tremendous encouragement for us.

Jesus gives us encouragement and His Spirit lives in us to fortify us. We read in Romans 15:5 that God gives us perseverance and encouragement. He knows we need to stay encouraged, and has made divine provision for us. We also have fellow Christians to keep us full of hope and courage. Paul tells us to encourage and build each other up (1 Thessalonians 5:11). We need both vertical connectedness with God and horizontal connectedness with each other.

There is another means of encouragement that we must have if we are to keep our hearts in step with His. We must learn to encourage ourselves in God. This is vital and it often goes overlooked and unlearned by us to our deep disadvantage. The best example I know of this form of heart encouragement is practiced by David.

In 1 Samuel 30:1-6, David and his army have finally hit bottom. They returned to Ziklag to find their homes burned to the ground and their wives and children kidnapped by the Amalekites. They were filled with sorrow, pain and remorse. David had a double discouragement because both of his wives and his entire family were in the hands of the enemy. His plight is deepened even further because his once loyal men, compelled by bitter disappointment, were now blaming him for their loss. Their conversation is one of great anger, and there is talk of stoning David.

David was having a horrible day. He was heartbroken, disappointed and his life was being threatened. There was nothing in his circumstances that produced courage or hope. The situation could not have been bleaker. God did not split the heavens, no angels visibly came to his rescue, and no human offered a word of consolation or comfort. Then we read these incredible words:

> *But David strengthened himself in the LORD his God. Then David said to Abiathar the priest, the son of Ahimelech, "Please bring me the ephod." So Abiathar brought the ephod to David. David inquired of the LORD, saying, "Shall I pursue this band? Shall I overtake them?" And He said to him, "Pursue, for you will surely overtake them, and you will surely rescue all"* (1 Samuel 30:6-8).

David was as down and depressed as he could be but he knew that God, and not his circumstances, ruled his life. This is a key element to encouraging yourself in God. You must actualize the faith and hope in your heart into action. David's faith was acting on what he knew to be true in spite of the circumstantial evidence that screamed to the contrary. He acted on the truth that God loved him, that the Lord was good and that He can be trusted. This brought him out to a place where he could be re-encouraged, hear from God, and respond accordingly.

The next thing David did was to get in God's presence. Even in the midst of all this trouble he knew where to go. He had the ephod of the High Priest brought to him which had the breast plate containing the Urim and Thummim. The Urim and Thummim were a divinely ordained means of communicating with God, and David put himself in a place and posture to speak to God and hear Him. He knew that revelation from the Lord was more important at this point than taking revenge or his own vindication.

This is so important. Look at David's focus. He did not focus on his loss or his enemies. He did not focus on the danger or the disappointment brought upon him by his men. His focus was solely on his Redeemer and Deliverer. His focus was on the Lord. And look what happened!

> *David slaughtered them from the twilight until the evening of the next day; and not a man of them escaped, except four hundred young men who rode on camels and fled. So David recovered all that the Amalekites had taken, and rescued his two wives. But nothing of theirs was missing, whether small or great, sons or daughters, spoil or anything that they had taken for themselves; David brought it all back. So David had captured all the sheep and the cattle which the people drove ahead of the other livestock, and they said, "This is David's spoil"* (1 Samuel 30:17-20).

David found that place of re-encouragement. He heard from God and acted on what he heard, resulting in great victory for his army and the restoration of all their wives, children and possessions. David had learned a valuable lesson. He found out how to re-encourage his heart before God and not simply live in defeat and despair.

How does that work? I think David knew what to do and where to go. I think he called to mind some of the Psalms, many of which he had written. Here are some other times David encouraged himself in the Lord.

> *The LORD is my light and my salvation; whom shall I fear? The LORD is the defense of my life; whom shall I dread? When evildoers came upon me to devour my flesh,*

my adversaries and my enemies, they stumbled and fell. Though a host encamp against me, my heart will not fear; though war arise against me, in spite of this I shall be confident (Psalm 27:1-3).

I will bless the Lord at all times; His praise shall continually be in my mouth. (Psalm 34:1).

Can you see what David is doing? He is "rehearsing" the truth in the presence of the circumstantial evidence. His heart declaration stems from his knowledge of the Father's heart. He declares to Himself the goodness and faithfulness of God.

O God, we have heard with our ears, our fathers have told us the work that You did in their days, in the days of old. You with Your own hand drove out the nations; then You planted them; You afflicted the peoples, then You spread them abroad. For by their own sword they did not possess the land, and their own arm did not save them, but Your right hand and Your arm and the light of Your presence, for You favored them. You are my King, O God; Command victories for Jacob. Through You we will push back our adversaries; through Your name we will trample down those who rise up against us. For I will not trust in my bow, nor will my sword save me. But You have saved us from our adversaries, and You have put to shame those who hate us. In God we have boasted all day long, and we will give thanks to Your name forever. Selah (Psalm 44:1-8).

Be gracious to me, O God, for man has trampled upon me; fighting all day long he oppresses me. My foes have trampled upon me all day long, for they are many who fight proudly against me. When I am afraid, I will put my trust in You (Psalm 56:1-3).

Bless God in the congregations, even the LORD, you who are of the fountain of Israel. Your God has commanded your strength; show Yourself strong, O God, who have acted on our behalf (Psalm 68:26, 28).

David called to mind that God was his light and his salvation, the defense of his life and his strong confidence. He recalled the times that God had delivered and rescued him from peril and death. He made God his strength and put his trust in the Lord in a present-tense fashion, knowing that his heavenly Father could command victory for him. He was afraid, so he did what he had done before when fear had him in its grip. He gave himself to God, concluding: What can mere men do to me? He acknowledged that God alone could command his strength (Psalm 68:28) and that God gives strength and power to him (Psalm 68:35).

Here are some lessons we can learn from this story that will help us when discouragement tries to beat down the door of our hearts.

First, we must always inquire of the Lord. When we regain our equilibrium, we must know whether we should pursue and fight or simply regroup and live to fight another day. Sometimes we will launch out like David did. Sometimes we will stay in the cave (David did this on occasion) waiting for new marching orders.

Secondly, you must know that God's presence and power can totally reverse a hostile situation. David's heart was strengthened and re-encouraged in God in such a mighty way that men who moments earlier wanted to kill him now risked their lives to follow him into battle. David received some kind of strengthening in God's presence. Something so real happened to him that it brought hope and courage to his army too. When we find ways to encourage ourselves in God it is not just for our benefit. It affects those around us as well.

Thirdly, David had 600 soldiers, but only 400 went into battle with him. The other 200 were too exhausted to make the trip (1 Samuel 30:9-10). Always recognize the connection between alignment and assignment. Always let the Lord pick your battles and your assignments. Two hundred of the men had not received strength and were ill-equipped to fight. Lack of commitment or lack of courage didn't keep these soldiers back. They simply did not have the physical energy and ability to fight at that level on that day. David was wise enough not to chastise them as cowards or try to use them as warriors. He simply treated them as friends and trusted God to win with the men who could fight. David's army easily won without the 200 men who stayed behind.

These men did not fight the battle, but they got their families and possessions restored to them too. Why? Because they had a leader and comrades that they knew and trusted, and who knew and trusted them. When you are able to strengthen yourself in God and get fresh encouragement in your heart, you can get God's perspectives and make wise choices. David and the 400 soldiers who fought not only had everything restored to them, but they also got to be agents of restoration to 200 of their closest friends. David came away with a strengthened relationship with God, and an army of men with a whole new level of respect for each other. His army was not only filled with new courage and strength, but with new gratitude and friendship.

We must learn to re-encourage our own hearts for the sake of our walk with Him and for the sake of those around us. "O Lord, teach me to strengthen and encourage myself in You!"

13

A Chosen Heart

Did you know that you are God's choice? Think about that for just a moment. The God of Heaven, the God who holds the whole universe together with His word of power has chosen you. When this truth settles in your heart, it gives you tremendous confidence to walk with Him, and genuine anticipation about the path of life that lies before you.

When I was very young, we used to play baseball every day, all summer long. A bunch of guys would get together and two of the oldest boys would be captains and choose teams. Although I didn't know it at that time, my eyesight was really poor and I had real trouble seeing the ball, which made me a lousy hitter. I was great at bunting and I was a good fielder but I was not good with the bat. This often led to me being one of the last guys chosen to play.

God is not like that. He chooses us based on what He can see in us, not based on how well we perform or produce. When your heart is established in His choice of you, then you can more readily comply and cooperate with His plans for you. The Word of God tells us about Him choosing us and it has some wonderful implications.

Peter, an apostle of Jesus Christ, To those who reside as aliens, scattered throughout Pontus, Galatia, Cappadocia, Asia, and Bithynia, who are chosen according to the foreknowledge of

God the Father, by the sanctifying work of the Spirit, to obey Jesus Christ and be sprinkled with His blood: May grace and peace be yours in the fullest measure. Blessed be the God and Father of our Lord Jesus Christ, who according to His great mercy has caused us to be born again to a living hope through the resurrection of Jesus Christ from the dead, to obtain an inheritance which is imperishable and undefiled and will not fade away, reserved in heaven for you, who are protected by the power of God through faith for a salvation ready to be revealed in the last time. In this you greatly rejoice, even though now for a little while, if necessary, you have been distressed by various trials (1 Peter 1:1-6).

Peter was writing to believers who had been dispersed all across Asia Minor. Some of them were in Jerusalem on the day of Pentecost. There was quite a contrast to being in a place where thousands were touched by God on Pentecost, with all the activity and miraculous momentum, and now being scattered about in distant places without all of that. Peter refers to them as aliens (v. 1) and I'm certain that they felt that way. We are all aliens in that we only reside here on earth temporarily, and are truly citizens of the kingdom of Heaven. We are aliens, but according to verse one, we are also chosen by God. It is a lot easier to walk out our time on earth with purpose and passion when we are certain of being chosen and destined by God *here*, and chosen to live forever with Him *there*. You have been chosen by God. How did God do that? Why has He chosen you? What bearing should this have on your life?

We are told that we are chosen by God's foreknowledge and the Spirit's sanctifying work in 1 Peter 1:1-2.

Peter, an apostle of Jesus Christ, to those who reside as aliens, scattered throughout Pontus, Galatia, Cappadocia, Asia, and Bithynia,who are chosen according to the foreknowledge of God the Father, by the sanctifying work of the Spirit, to obey Jesus Christ and be sprinkled with His blood: May grace and peace be yours in the fullest measure.

Foreknowledge means you see before and have advanced or predetermined knowledge. The Greek word is *prognosis*. The Great Physician knew in advance that we were all dying of this sickness called sin, so He applied the only remedy that would cure us—the cross of Jesus Christ. This brought the solution to our sin problem.

God foreknew that our sin would separate us from Him. The declaration of His heart is clear. He wants no one to perish and He wants everyone to come to the knowledge of the truth (2 Peter 3:9). So He sends the Holy Spirit to draw us unto Himself (John 6:44) that we might be freed to say *yes* to His choice of us by giving our lives to Him. God's Spirit sets us apart for this sanctifying process so that we can be His (1 Thessalonians 5:23, 2 Thessalonians 2:13).

Why did He choose you? This is an amazing statement: He chose you so you could be free to obey. 1 Peter 1:2 says, *"We are chosen...to obey Jesus Christ and be sprinkled by His blood."* You have been chosen by God to obey and be cleansed and forgiven. You have been chosen to be able to obey Him. The idea of being chosen means that you are chosen "unto" obedience or chosen resulting in obedience (Romans 5:16, Romans 16:25-27, John 15:16).

Obedience always involves our volition. We always have to make the decision to obey but that decision becomes a much clearer option when we realize that He chose us to be able to obey. Obedience is not just a product of discipline or determination, it is part of your DNA. When a living knowledge of God's choice of you beats in your heart, then your choice of Him in any given situation (obedience) is a *natural* response and in fact it is your desired response. Does this mean you will always say *yes* to God and never disobey? Of course not, but it does mean that obedience is a normal flow of thought for you, and something you can always want to do.

You have been chosen by God to obey God. This means that you receive empowerment from God to help you enforce your decision (Romans 6:16-19, Colossians 3:12-17). Don't you think that if God chose you for a purpose that He will help you fulfill that purpose? Sure He will, because that is what God is like. Paul tells us as much in Philippians 2:13, *"For it is God who is at work in you, both to will and to work for His good pleasure."*

He will inform you about what it means to obey Him in a situation, and then lead you in ways that cause obedience to become a very viable choice. If He chose you to sing or speak, or go to a foreign country to minister, wouldn't you expect His help in carrying out your actions? Simple obedience in life situations is no different, especially when you know that you were born again to be able to obey Him.

God saves you, forgives you, and frees you to say *yes* to Him for His glory and for your benefit, and the benefit of others. You are freed from the slavery of sin (disobedience) so you can present yourself to Him and be obedient from the heart (Romans 6:17-18).

You become saved by making your choice of Jesus Christ as your Lord and Savior, but this is only the beginning. God's choice of you was not just so you could be saved and go to Heaven. His choice of you was to set you apart to be able to obey Him freely for the rest of your life. It deeply honors Him when you face situations where you can make any decision you want, and you choose obedience. It is my conviction that every time you chose obedience when you could go in several other directions, you rub the devil's nose in the dirt. The devil never concluded that sinful humans, when offered all the options, would consistently choose to obey. He didn't make that choice, and I think that he is confounded when you do.

The Lord chose you once and forever so that you might knowingly make the choice to obey Him. Obedience is the outflow of a heart that knows God's choice and fully desires to comply by saying *yes* to Him. Are you aware that you concur with and fulfill the will of God each time that you make the choice to obey? The heart that is joined to God's heart knows the call to obey and the Holy Spirit works within to make obedience a re-occurring reality.

"O God, show me that you have chosen me for the purpose of obedience. Let your Spirit stir within me to help me comply with Your will."

14

A Hearing Heart

What thoughts come to your mind when someone says, "God told me something" or "I heard from the Lord?" Are you curious? Envious? Skeptical?

I have been in ministry for decades and one of the most common subjects of conversation involves the concept of hearing from God. People come to me because they question what they have heard from God. They don't think they can hear from Him or hope that I am able to hear from Him.

Our ability to walk with Him, obey Him and fulfill our purposes in Him hinge on having a heart that hears from Him. Jesus tells us, *"Man shall not live on bread alone, but on every word that proceeds out of the mouth of God"* (Matthew 4:4). Like the manna the children of Israel lived on in the wilderness, we need to live on the word of the Lord. We cannot live the life we are called to without it.

This is good news because if we must have this *proceeding* word from God to live on, it means that He is most assuredly speaking it. Since He speaks it and it is a necessity that we have it, then our heart can certainly hear and receive it. One of the central ways we know what is on God's heart is to discern what is coming from His mouth.

We never want to confuse the word of the Lord that proceeds today from His lips with the written Word of God. The

Bible is the written Word of the Lord and it does not change. It is settled forever in Heaven (Psalm 119:89). I like to say it like this, "The Bible is God's Word and it is the Word He has said to us. The word of the Lord is what He is saying in the present-tense about what He has already said. The Word of God is a lamp and a light to us and we never outgrow our dependence upon it, our need for it or our delight in it. God graciously gives us His *proceeding* word to guide, encourage and teach us to understand and obey the Word."

Jesus is our good shepherd, and He knows the sheep of His flock, and we know Him. Jesus' familiar words in John 10 are very revealing and helpful in this matter.

> *My sheep hear My voice, and I know them, and they follow Me; and I give eternal life to them, and they will never perish; and no one will snatch them out of My hand* (John 10:27-28).

> *But he who enters by the door is a shepherd of the sheep. To him the doorkeeper opens, and the sheep hear his voice, and he calls his own sheep by name and leads them out. When he puts forth all his own, he goes ahead of them, and the sheep follow him because they know his voice* (John 10:2-4).

> *I am the good shepherd, and I know My own and My own know Me, even as the Father knows Me and I know the Father; and I lay down My life for the sheep* (John 10:14-15).

He knows us. He calls us by name. We know Him and He speaks to us. Hearing the voice of the Lord is a most normal and needful experience. It is one of the key elements in having a heart that beats with His heart and follows Him. Seven times in Revelation Jesus says, *"He who has an ear, let him hear what the Spirit says to the churches."* This was spoken directly to the seven churches but it certainly applies to us today.

God has always wanted His people to hear His voice. We have such a terrific advantage of having His Spirit living in us to help us hear and respond. We do have an *ear* and we can hear from God. Have you ever read these words from the book of Jeremiah?

For I did not speak to your fathers, or command them in the day that I brought them out of the land of Egypt, concerning burnt offerings and sacrifices. But this is what I commanded them, saying, "Obey My voice, and I will be your God, and you will be My people; and you will walk in all the way which I command you, that it may be well with you." Yet they did not obey or incline their ear, but walked in their own counsels and in the stubbornness of their evil heart, and went backward and not forward (Jeremiah 7:22-24).

There are amazing statements hidden in these verses. God says that He did not bring their fathers out of Egypt to get offerings and sacrifices from them. (They sure did a lot of that!) His commandment to them was for them to obey His voice, so that He would be their God and they would be His people, and that it may be well with them. God's desire for His people was and is that we obey His voice. This means that He does speak and we can hear Him. Our communing and communicating with Him establishes a deepening relationship (we are His people and He is our God) and it shows us the way to be led by Him and to obey Him. This issue of connecting, communicating and relating to God has always been on His heart and it is His desire for us today. A heart in rhythm with God's heart is a hearing heart.

Jesus makes this heart matter abundantly clear in these verses from the Gospel of John:

"These things I have spoken to you while abiding with you. But the Helper, the Holy Spirit, whom the Father will send in My name, He will teach you all things, and bring to your remembrance all that I said to you" (John 14:25-26).

"I have many more things to say to you, but you cannot bear them now. But when He, the Spirit of truth, comes, He will guide you into all the truth; for He will not speak on His own initiative, but whatever He hears, He will speak; and He will disclose to you what is to come. He will glorify Me, for He will take of Mine and will disclose it to you. All things that the Father has are Mine; therefore I said that He takes of Mine and will disclose it to you" (John 16:12-15).

The Holy Spirit has been sent to us and into us to teach us to hear God's voice and to receive the *proceeding* word from Heaven. He will teach us all we need to know and remind us of things we have read in the Word or have already heard from the Lord (John 14:26). He will teach, lead and instruct us in God's Word and God's ways. He enables us to hear and to respond to what we hear.

Jesus tells His disciples that He had a lot more to teach and tell them, but they simply couldn't handle it without the Holy Spirit's help. The disciples had not yet received the indwelling Spirit and did not receive Him until after Jesus' resurrection (John 20:22). He does tell them that when the Holy Spirit comes to them that the Spirit will guide them into all the truth. In fact, Jesus tells them that whatever He tells the Holy Spirit, the Holy Spirit will speak to them. He will even disclose to them things yet to come (John 16:13). The Holy Spirit taught and led the disciples by speaking to their hearts. (He didn't just use "sign" language!) We need to be taught, trained and led by God's voice at least as much as His disciples were. The Spirit of God spoke to them and He is speaking to us today. We must believe it and allow Him to develop a hearing heart within us.

God speaks to us because He is a good Father who loves and disciplines His children.

> *Has any people heard the voice of God speaking from the midst of the fire, as you have heard it, and survived? ....To you it was shown that you might know that the LORD, He is God; there is no other besides Him. Out of the heavens He let you hear His voice to discipline you; and on earth He let you see His great fire, and you heard His words from the midst of the fire* (Deuteronomy 4:33, 35-36).

We see from these words that God speaks to assure us of who He is, and to assure us that we *are* His. He speaks to us to confirm His love for us and His deep desire for relationship with us. He wants our confidence to be in Him and our love to be for Him. He speaks to us to solidify this truth—*"I am my beloveds and He is mine"* (Song of Solomon 6:3).

The Lord's voice should impact our hearts and lives. Regardless of the situations we face or the opportunities that we encounter, the Lord desires to reveal His will, His way and His good pleasure. Isaiah has some excellent instructions concerning God speaking His wisdom to us.

> *Give ear and hear my voice, Listen and hear my words. Does the farmer plow continually to plant seed? Does he continually turn and harrow the ground? Does he not level its surface and sow dill and scatter cummin and plant wheat in rows, barley in its place and rye within its area? For his God instructs and teaches him properly....This also comes from the LORD of hosts, who has made His counsel wonderful and His wisdom great* (Isaiah 28:23-26, 29).

The Lord exhorts us to listen to His voice and to hear His words. He instructs us in this passage about times and seasons and tells us that He has made His counsel wonderful and His wisdom great! (Isaiah 29:29). How does His counsel and wisdom come? It comes as we give ear to His voice and listen to His words, *"Listen and hear my voice; pay attention and hear what I say"* (Isaiah 28:23).

I read this passage some time ago and this is what I heard the Lord saying to me: "Do not let the length or the strength of the season that you are in deceive or deter you. I will speak to you and instruct you properly."

Let that be an encouragement to you (it certainly was to me in that moment) and let it serve as a simple example of the *proceeding* word that He speaks to us.

The Lord wants to produce an ever-developing heart that hears from Him. It is part of His gift to us in the person of the Holy Spirit. If you are skilled in hearing God's voice, I encourage you to carry on and grow even deeper. If you are just beginning to hear His voice, then press on and don't give up. If you don't feel like you hear from God, then please call out for His help. Go back through this chapter and read the scripture references again and pray them out to God. He is speaking and He doesn't want your heart to be cheated from hearing His voice.

15

A Commanded Heart

The Bible tells us that, *"The wise of heart receive a command..."* (Proverbs 10:8). Immediately this causes us to think of being willingly obedient and compliant to God's Word. Such obedience is a desirable and necessary characteristic, but it is not that type of a command that I want to examine here. I want to look at some things that our hearts must believe and accept that God has commanded for us, not to obey, but to receive.

Have your eyes ever rested on these wonderful words from Psalm 42? *"The LORD will command His loving kindness in the daytime; And His song will be with me in the night, A prayer to the God of my life"* (Psalm 42:8).

I am so glad God does not just suggest or recommend His loving kindness for me. No, He *commands* His loving kindness. He sends forth His loving kindness in a way that accomplishes His commanded purpose. When He commands something, it happens!

Think of some of the issues about which the Lord has issued commandments.

"Let there be light, and there was light" (Genesis 1:3).

"No longer shall your name be Abram, but your name shall be Abraham; for I will make you the father of a multitude of nations" (Genesis 16:5).

"He cried out with a loud voice 'Lazarus come forth.' And he who had died came forth..." (John 11:43).

"And the blind man said to him 'Rabboni, I want to regain my sight!' And Jesus said to him, 'Go your way; your faith has made you well'" (Mark 10:51-52).

Some pretty amazing things occurred when the Lord, in His loving kindness, commanded from His heart for those He loved. We need to obey the commands of scripture and we need to benefit from His commanded goodness to us. Our hearts must be attuned to the incredible love in God's heart toward us. We cannot be all wrapped up in trying to earn His favor or perform our way to spiritual rewards. God in His kindness simply chooses to release His riches to us and we must have a well-tuned heart response to receive it. You do not see Abraham, Lazarus or Bartimaeus trying to manipulate God for something more or refuse His touch due to their unworthiness. They simply opened their hearts and said *yes* and *thank you!*

It is difficult to over-estimate the power of a commanded heart. We read in Psalm 68:28, *"Your God has commanded your strength; Show Yourself strong, O God, who have acted on our behalf."*

Our God has commanded our strength! Don't you love that? He wants us to grow in grace and exercise our faith, but He also commands strength for us. Joel 3:10 says it this way, *"Let the weak say I am a mighty man."* One translation puts it like this, *"Let the weak say I am a warrior"* (Joel 3:10, An American Translation). You can just sense something building and rising up within you when your heart is empowered by such powerful proclamations. The Lord has commanded His loving-kindness toward us, which infuses us with strength, so that in the midst of weakness we can declare that we have a warrior's heart.

There is a magnificent unfolding of God's heart toward us in this regard in Psalm 44:3-7.

For by their own sword they did not possess the land, And their own arm did not save them, But Your right hand and Your arm and the light of Your presence, For You favored them. You are my King, O God; Command victories for Jacob.

Through You we will push back our adversaries; Through
Your name we will trample down those who rise up against
us. For I will not trust in my bow, Nor will my sword save
me. But You have saved us from our adversaries, And You
have put to shame those who hate us. In God we have boasted
all day long, And we will give thanks to Your name forever.
Selah (Psalm 44:1-8).

God commands loving kindness toward us. He proclaims
the strength of a warrior's heart in us and then declares commanded victories for us - His right hand, His strong arm and
the light of His presence. This three-faceted favor of God results in commanded victories for us. What a wealth of encouragement and fuel for faith, God's commanded victory!

He intended for us to walk with Him with a heart that readily responds to the commands of His Word and with a heart
that also readily receives His commanded blessings.

Behold, how good and how pleasant it is for brothers to dwell
together in unity! It is like the precious oil upon the head,
coming down upon the beard, even Aaron's beard, coming
down upon the edge of his robes. It is like the dew of Hermon
coming down upon the mountains of Zion; for there the Lord
commanded the blessing—life forever (Psalm 133:1-3).

There truly is a commanded blessing of life forever! Jesus
commands everlasting life for us. He commands abundant
life for us - a life that is in union with Him and unity with
each other. A life in unity with Him flows with His goodness
and overflows with His favor, blessing, strength and loving
kindness. When our heart beats with things like this, God is
honored, the Kingdom is proclaimed, and we are fulfilled.
Commanded blessing, commanded loving kindness, and commanded strength that results in commanded victory—these
are the rhythms of a captured heart.

16

The Scarlet Letter

There is something amazing about the power of pardon. We pass over familiar words like forgiveness and pardon and our hearts are not significantly impacted by what has been so magnificently accomplished for us. I think that the Lord desires for us to have our hearts and minds imprinted with the reality of this issue of being pardoned.

Have you ever read *The Scarlet Letter*? The following is an overview:

The Scarlet Letter follows the public shaming and punishment of a young woman named Hester Prynne in mid-17th century Boston (a.k.a. the Massachusetts Bay Colony). When Hester becomes pregnant, everyone believes her to be guilty of adultery: she has been separated from her husband for two full years, and the baby cannot be his. The magistrates (local law enforcers) and ministers order her to wear a scarlet letter "A" on the bodice of her dress, so that everyone can know about her adultery.

The Scarlet Letter begins when Hester is briefly released from prison so that she can be paraded through town, displaying her scarlet "A" while standing on top of the town scaffold (a public stage). She carries her baby daughter, Pearl, in her arms. Pearl was born in prison. Hester steadfastly refuses to reveal the name of Pearl's father, so that he might be saved from punishment.

Hester Prynne's long lost husband arrives in the midst of this parade through town. He visits her in prison before her release and asks her not to tell anyone that he's in town. His plan is to disguise himself so that he can ferret out and seek revenge on her lover.

Hester's husband tells the townspeople that he's a physician, and he adopts a fake name: Roger Chillingworth. Hester keeps his secret. Chillingworth soon realizes that the minister, the Reverend Arthur Dimmesdale, is the likely father of Hester's baby, and he haunts the minister's mind and soul, day and night, for the next seven years.

The minister is too afraid to confess his sin publicly, but his guilt eats away at him; Chillingworth's constant examination really makes him antsy. Seven years pass and, finally, Hester realizes the evil her husband has done to the man she loves, the father of her child. She reveals Chillingworth's true identity to Dimmesdale, and the two concoct a plan to leave Boston and go to England, where they might hide from Hester's husband and create a new life together.

The minister is ultimately unable to go through with the plan. Dimmesdale confesses his sin to the townspeople on the scaffold that had, seven years earlier, been the scene of Hester's public shaming. His dying act is to throw open his shirt so that the scarlet A that he has carved onto his chest is revealed to his parishioners. Dimmesdale finds peace through confession.

When Chillingworth dies approximately a year after his rival, Dimmesdale, he leaves all his money and property to Pearl. Hester and Pearl finally escape the community where they have been outcasts for so many years and return to the Old World (a.k.a. England). However, many years later, Hester returns to the New England community that had been the site of her shame, resuming the scarlet letter of her own will.

When she dies, she is buried near the minister, and they share a gravestone. The gravestone contains an image, described as follows: "On a field, sable, the letter A, gules." In other words, marked on the headstone is a scarlet letter A drawn over a black background.

My experience tells me that too many Christians wear the "mark" of their sins, failures and shortcomings of the past. We walk in the shadows of those things and they influence and affect us more than the reality of God's pardon. It is essential that we overcome this for our hearts to beat with His.

Paul gives us some tremendous help in Colossians:

> *When you were dead in your transgressions and the uncircumcision of your flesh, He made you alive together with Him, having forgiven us all our transgressions, having canceled out the certificate of debt consisting of decrees against us, which was hostile to us; and He has taken it out of the way, having nailed it to the cross. When He had disarmed the rulers and authorities, He made a public display of them, having triumphed over them through Him* (Colossians 2:13-16).

What a terrific solution to dealing with sin, doubt and failure! Jesus took all the accusations, condemnations and the certificate of our debt decreed against us and nailed it to the cross. Enough said, case closed! (Colossians 2:14). He has dealt with the devil's schemes and wants us to live "debt-free!" The enemy would love to entangle us with elementary and worldly principles (so we can salve the ache of our conscience and justify our failures). We impose our self-made religious rights and bodily restraints rather than walk in the freedom that the cross provides for us (Colossians 2:20-23).

I heard a story years ago that speaks to the issue at hand. A man in a horse-drawn cart happened upon a woman walking down the road. The woman was carrying a heavy load and was bent under the weight of her burden. The man stopped and offered her a ride. She gratefully accepted his offer and sat down in an empty space in the small cart. The man drove on for a mile or so and then looked back to check on his passenger. He turned to see how the lady was doing and could not believe his eyes. The woman was contentedly in his cart but her burden was still on her back. She was relieved from the work of the walk but not from the weight of what she was carrying.

Do you see anything in that simple story? The Lord has used that story countless times to help me help me illustrate to others why they find it so hard to press on in this life. Jesus not only accepts us, He takes the weight that sin piles on us. He takes the effect of our sins and the sins of others against us, so that we can realize all that His death and resurrection brings to us. The woman in this story was not being humble by continuing to "shoulder the load," she was living a misunderstanding of what grace is. It honors the Lord to receive the full blessing of His sacrificial death for us. He embraces us and the load that the world, the flesh and the devil have brought our way.

David shows us the Lord's heart on this matter in Psalm 28:9: *"Save your people and bless your inheritance; be their shepherd and carry them forever."*

God's heart towards us is to release us from the pressure of sin, guilt and shame. He wants us free to live with Him, walk with Him and free to fulfill our destiny in Him. The woman in the story would reach her destination because the cart carried her there, but the journey was not nearly what the cart owner had planned for her. The Lord, like the man in the story, is very interested in enabling you to reach the destination that He has for you (Eternity with Him). He is as interested in the lives we live each day, as He is in our being with Him in Heaven.

It is vital that we accept His invitation to us for eternal life. It is equally as significant that we give Him all that would hinder us from following Him fully in the lives He has given us here and now. Our identity must be based on who He is in us, who we are in Him and what He has done for us. His presence truly is more powerful than our past. The things we have done, failed to do, or experienced are no match for what He has done on our behalf.

The enemy has never experienced pardon, so he simply can't comprehend the depth of release and gratitude that God's pardon brings to us. It might be healthy to envision a large "P" imprinted on your shirt, a blood-red "P" that signifies our blood-bought pardon. Let that "mark" your thinking and help influence how you see yourself. Mercy triumphs over judgment. Amen!

17

Ministering to the Lord

There is a powerful heart-principle that we can learn from the sons of Zadok. Zadok served along with Abiathar as a priest under David. His sons were remarkably faithful to the Lord at a time when the other Levitical priests strayed in their hearts and in their service.

The Levites who departed from the Lord and served idols were only allowed to minister in the house of the Lord and to the people (Ezekiel 44:9-14). They were not given access to minister to the Lord Himself. The right to minister to the Lord was reserved for the sons of Zadok whose heart remained true to God through the years.

"But the Levitical priests, the sons of Zadok, who kept charge of My sanctuary when the sons of Israel went astray from Me, shall come near to Me to minister to Me; and they shall stand before Me to offer Me the fat and the blood," declares the Lord GOD. "They shall enter My sanctuary; they shall come near to My table to minister to Me and keep My charge. It shall be that when they enter at the gates of the inner court, they shall be clothed with linen garments; and wool shall not be on them while they are ministering in the gates of the inner court and in the house. Linen turbans shall be on their heads and linen undergarments shall be on their loins; they

*shall not gird themselves with anything which makes them
sweat. When they go out into the outer court, into the outer court to the people, they shall put off their garments in
which they have been ministering and lay them in the holy
chambers; then they shall put on other garments so that they
will not transmit holiness to the people with their garments"*
(Ezekiel 44:15-19).

The sons of Zadok were granted a tremendous privilege
because of their faithfulness to the Lord. They were given entrance to the inner court (a picture of spiritual intimacy). They
were given linen turbans for their heads (a symbol of the renew-
ing of the mind) and linen undergarments (linen represents the
spiritual body). They wore nothing that would cause sweat (a
picture of ministry in the Spirit and not in the flesh). They were
enabled to minister to the Lord and to be powerfully impacted
by His presence. The presence of God was so powerful that
the clothing they wore in the inner courts had to be stored in
a place separate from where the people entered the temple because their clothing would transmit holiness if it were touched.
If their clothing was so saturated by His presence, what do you
suppose happened to their hearts and minds? What a blessing!
What a privilege! What a wonderful illustration for us!

We now live under a better covenant with better promises.
We have a new and living way to access God's presence (Hebrews 4:16). We can boldly come into His presence by virtue
of the finished work of His Son residing in us. What a tremendous benefit and motivation to go before God and worship
Him, praise Him and minister to Him. What a challenge to live
before Him in such a way that our very lives would provoke
people to righteousness and goodness when we come into contact with them.

Think for a moment, we now live with a better covenant
with better promises than these priests were given. How much
better is better? They had the blessing of ministering to God
and even their clothing was saturated with holiness!

This has some incredible implications for us. We are told
that we are a Royal Priesthood and that we are to proclaim the
excellencies of Him who has called us out of darkness and into
His marvelous light (1 Peter 2:9). He has given us an unlimited

capacity to enter into His presence, and we can love Him, offer our lives to Him be an honor to Him, and a light to the world around us. Amazing! This blessing is no longer restricted to a select group of priests, but is open to all believers who trust the name of Jesus. Let us be faithful to come before His throne and bless His magnificent name.

One of the tremendous benefits of ministering to the Lord like the sons of Zadok was the effect it had on their understanding of God's heart. In Ezekiel 44:23, we read that they were able to teach God's people the difference between the holy and the profane. They were also empowered to train people to discern between the clean and the unclean. They had been touched by the Lord and instructed in their hearts to know what pleased Him, and to know how to choose the things that delighted and honored Him.

Oh that our lives would declare to those around us what blesses and brings glory to the heart of God! What a magnificent ministry this is, to be able to equip the saints to bring honor and glory to the Father. If we can grow in God and mature in ways that impart that kind of wisdom and discipline to His people, then we are walking in the priesthood to which He has called us.

Paul understood this vital aspect of waiting before the Lord and devoting his time and affection to Him:

> *While they were ministering to the Lord and fasting, the Holy Spirit said, "Set apart for Me Barnabas and Saul for the work to which I have called them." Then, when they had fasted and prayed and laid their hands on them, they sent them away. So, being sent out by the Holy Spirit, they went down to Seleucia and from there they sailed to Cyprus* (Acts 13:2-4).

Paul and his partners were praying, fasting and ministering to the Lord at Antioch. In the midst of blessing and pursuing God, the voice of the Lord communicated His choice and calling of Barnabas and Paul. This time of offering themselves to the Lord and focusing on the desire of His heart released God's purpose for Paul and Barnabas, and for the church at Antioch.

There is nothing in this scripture to indicate that the purpose of this presence-filled session was to find His will for their ministry. The Lord simply chose this opportunity to illustrate a vital truth for us. When we fix our gaze and our intent on loving and bringing honor to Him, then He releases His heart for us to us. They assembled to minister to the Lord and the Lord seized the opportunity to profoundly reveal His direction to them.

We must be a people who will move ourselves to a place of worship and devotion to God, knowing that God will move upon us to make His heart known to us in due season. The declaration of God's purposes for Paul and Barnabas was not the reason for ministering to the Lord, just the inevitable result. Devotion to Him in our hearts brings a revelation of our destiny to our understanding. Bless the Lord!

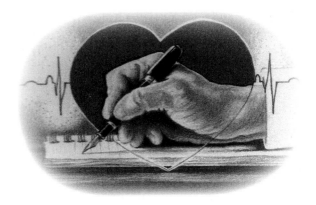

18

Passing Under the Rod

Americans have been raised with a concept referred to as the *American Dream*. This platitude encompasses a number of things, but one central theme is to own your own home. Ownership is an important issue to us. We all want our own home. God is not an American, but I have come to understand that ownership is an important theme to Him as well.

I had this point of God's ownership impressed upon my heart in a peculiar way. Some things stirred in me when I read "pass under the rod." Those words *leaped* off the page and into my understanding.

> *"For every tenth part of herd or flock, whatever passes under the rod, the tenth one shall be holy to the Lord"* (Leviticus 27:32).

> *"'In the cities of the hill country... the flocks will again pass under the hands of the one who numbers them,' says the Lord"* (Jeremiah 33:13).

> *"And I will cause you to pass under the rod [as the shepherd does his sheep when he counts them, and I will count you as Mine and I will constrain you] and bring you into the covenant to which you are permanently bound"* (Ezekiel 20:37, Amplified Bible).

Shepherds of days past would stand in the sheep pen and cause each sheep to pass single-file before him. He would have a rod saturated in vermilion (a bright red pigment) and mark every tenth animal as a tithe to the Lord. This signified God's ownership of the entire flock and of every tenth sheep in particular.

When I read the words "pass under the rod," I knew that the Lord was inviting me to do just that. He has already purchased me. I belong to Him. We see this in 1 Corinthians 6:20, "For you have been bought with a price, therefore glorify God in your body," and in 1 Corinthians 7:23, "You were bought with a price; don't become slaves of men."

He had purchased me with the blood of His Son and it was a fresh opportunity for me to acknowledge His ownership of me and my dedication to Him. I could hear from Heaven in my heart. I heard that when you pass under the rod you can take nothing with you. Your pedigree or stature means nothing. The only thing that matters is that you are a sheep of His flock and that you are marked by the blood of the Lamb. He graciously permitted me to pass under His rod that day, and I have no doubt that He is my God and I belong to Him for His purposes.

I love the way that the Amplified Bible translates Ezekiel 20:37: *["And I will count you as Mine and I will constrain you] and bring you into the covenant to which you are permanently bound."*

The Lord says, *"I will count you as Mine."* Listen, when He counts you as His then you really do count. You matter to Him *big-time* and you cannot tell yourself or let the enemy tell you that you don't. His ownership of us is sure, powerful and purposeful. It means that He will direct us, correct us and instruct us in how to live in covenant love with Him and with others. It means that when we yield to Him, and humbly *pass under the rod* before Him, He will bring us into the manifold richness of belonging to Him.

I read these verses and responded to God from my heart. I said *yes* in the most sincere fashion that I knew how. I penned this little poem as a token of my heart response to Him.

Pass Under the Rod
Ezekiel 20:37, Leviticus 27:32, Jeremiah 33:13

Pass under the rod, pass under the rod
Do not refuse the hand of your Father
Do not ignore the call of your God
Pass under the rod, pass under the rod.

Pass under the rod, pass under the rod
Come unto Him, the One who numbers
The sheep gate is narrow, the pasture is broad
Pass under the rod, pass under the rod

Pass under the rod, pass under the rod
His rod is like a plumb-line dropped
When it has gone forth, it cannot be stopped
Pass under the rod, pass under the rod.

The Lord takes this issue of our passing under the rod and His ownership of us seriously, and He wants us to be serious about these matters as well. When our heart beats with His on this issue, then abiding in Him and He in us becomes even sweeter and more natural.

I see another expression of this concept of God's ownership of us and His residing within us in the Psalms. I was reading Psalm 132 one day when a little song burst forth from me. *"Surely I will not enter my house, Nor lie on my bed; I will not give sleep to my eyes or slumber to my eyelids, Until I find a place for the Lord, a dwelling place for the Mighty One of Jacob"* (Psalm 132:3-5).

I innocently sang these verses to the Lord in a simple melody that was dancing in my head, but they had a profound influence on my heart. He did not want me to operate in the status quo; He did not want me to conduct business as usual. He did not want me to *rest* until I found a place *in me* for Him to feel *at home.* The Psalmist says that he won't rest until he finds a dwelling place for the Lord. God wants to build a home for Himself in me. I know that God's Spirit lives in me, but He doesn't want to live like a guest when He owns the whole house. I was bought with a price. He owns me and my life is His, which includes my body. My body is His temple,

His dwelling place. He is the owner. I simply live here *rent-free*!

I knew the theological truths that I am discussing here, but the Lord made them personal to me. I determined that day to release myself to Him in any way He deemed acceptable so that He could feel at home in my life. He wants to make His home in me and exert His rights, and the authority of ownership in my life. (He also exercises the protection and provision of ownership!)

Have you "passed under the rod"? Is the red mark of ownership obvious to you? Is the Lord *at home* living in you? Does your heart beat with His on these issues? It can and He desires it to be so.

"Lord, have Your place in me. Dwell in me. Live in me. Love in me. Rule in me."

19

The Apostolic Attribute: Patience with Joy

I have found that the Lord is amazingly wise, wonderful, and loving. But I have also found out that among His other inscrutable attributes there is one I never would have guessed. In fact, only as I have increased in the knowledge of His ways has this discovery been made fully real to me. God is, and I say this with all reverence and honor, incredibly subversive! He displays His astute subversiveness in a variety of ways. I would like to examine one of them in this chapter.

The Lord *plants* truths for us in His Word so we might come to know Him and understand Him more accurately. I have found that we can greatly benefit from studying and applying the prayers we find recorded in scripture. I also found an illustration of His subversiveness (which I had not yet seen) as I innocently read Paul's prayer:

> *For this reason also, since the day we heard of it, we have not ceased to pray for you and to ask that you may be filled with the knowledge of His will in all spiritual wisdom and understanding, so that you will walk in a manner worthy of the Lord, to please Him in all respects, bearing fruit in every good work and increasing in the knowledge of God; strengthened with all power, according to His glorious might, for the attaining of all steadfastness and patience; joyously giving thanks to the Father, who has qualified us to share in the inheritance of*

the saints in light (Colossians 1:9-12).

Have you ever meditated on Paul's prayer for the church at Colosse? It is filled with terrific ammunition for your prayer gun. There are great riches to be gained from praying these words that pour forth from Paul's heart for the Colossians. There is also a surprise ending to the prayer - a *back-door* blessing that caught me quite off-guard. God is great and God is subversive.

Let's take a look at Paul's prayer. He begins in Colossians 1:9 by praying that these believers might be *"filled with the knowledge of His will in all spiritual wisdom and understanding."* What a request! Paul knew how vital it was for Christians to have a real knowledge, and a true revelation of the character and nature of God. He knew that spiritual wisdom and insight were crucial for them to grow and mature in their walk with God.

Wisdom and knowledge of who God is are essential but not just for the sake of having a correct perspective. Paul expands his prayer in Colossians 1:10 to tell us the purpose for having a genuine understanding of God's heart. It is to empower believers to walk out their faith. It is to live a life that is *worthy* of a Christ-follower and to bring pleasure to Him. Honoring God everyday and in every way is of prime importance, and is one reason that Paul prays for Christians as he does.

He also prays that the Colossians would be fruitful in every good work. Paul knew that people who learned to love God and glorify Him in their daily walk must also find ways to give their lives away to those around them. He wanted them to bear fruit through blessing and serving others, which would also result in others being helped and finding the Lord for themselves (Colossians 1:10). Interestingly, He also prays that as a result of their good works they would come to know God even better. Paul prays that Christians would come to know and love God more and give their love to others, which in turn would cause them to know and love God even more. What a virtuous cycle of cause and effect!

The words of Paul in Colossians 1:11 are astounding and lead to a profound and surprising climax. He prays that these Christians would be *"strengthened with all power according to His glorious might"* (Colossians 1:11). Paul is praying for divine empowerment, for a Holy Spirit fortified strength and for a power infusion for the church. What a daunting task! What incredible challenge awaited the Colossians that would require such a deepening of power and strength? The answer to this question might surprise you, and it certainly got my attention. The reasons given by Paul for praying this, along with the next part of his prayer, are simply these: he prays for the attainment of all steadfastness and patience joyously. (In verse 12 he adds the request for an attitude of gratitude.)

This is the subversive element to Paul's prayer. He prays for wisdom, knowledge and revelation for them. He prays for an enduement of strength and power for them. This wisdom, knowledge, revelation and power he prays for is all for the purpose of the Colossians having great patience with joy. He doesn't just pray for patience attended with joy. No, he is insightful enough to know that genuine patience requires real spiritual wisdom and revelation in the knowledge of Jesus, and enduring, empowered strength from the Lord. Patience of the kind required to see things through, patience that endures to see all God's purposes prevail, must be born of revelatory insight and fueled by Holy Spirit power.

This is brilliant! Paul prays for the Colossians to have wisdom, knowledge, fruitful expression of ministry and spiritual power and strength so that patience could be theirs. Patience with joy and gratitude would be the answer to Paul's prayer. You would think that the end result of such prayers, and the goal of his request, would be revival or some visitation of God's power. No, Paul knew patience would be necessary and that human grit and zeal would never produce it. Only a God-energized encounter of wisdom and strength could bring the kind of patience people would need to make the *long haul*.

Do you see the subversive element here? The Lord does not have Paul pray for patience alone for the church. Most people would lose patience praying for patience. He compels Paul to pray for all these wonderful things that come from encountering Him, because it is through the outworking of these things that God can birth and nurture patience in us. Very coy, very tricky, very subversive, very wise!

None of us have a problem when God shows up in the

now. We all love it when He suddenly comes to His temple. The Lord knows us and He knows that it is by faith and patience we receive God's promises (Hebrews 10:35-36).

I encourage you to pray Paul's prayer found in Colossians 1:9-12 and receive this God empowered attribute of patience in your life. Paul lived with this apostolic level of patience that was birthed in His heart from Heaven and God's pleasure would be to see it birthed and growing in us.

20

The Timelessly Well-Timed Heart

One of the foundational truths that you get from reading the Bible is that human beings are created in the image of God. (See Genesis 1:27) I am not certain about all the implications of this reality, but it is certain that there is something in His heart that responds to us, and something in our hearts that senses a need for Him.

Paul describes God like this in 1 Timothy 1:17: "Now to the King eternal, immortal, invisible, the only God, be honor and glory forever and ever, Amen."

We are created in the image of this immortal, invisible and eternal king. What does that mean and what does that look like? How are we as humans supposed to comprehend and respond to an eternal, immortal God who also just happens to be invisible?

I think these words from Solomon can help us grasp this concept more thoroughly.

Ecclesiastes 3:11 (Amplified Bible) *"He has made everything beautiful in its time. He has also set eternity in the human heart; yet no one can fathom what God has done from beginning to end."*

God has placed eternity in the heart of every person. He has put an eternal "ache" in each heart, not eternal life. Eternal life only comes by placing your faith in Jesus as your Savior and Lord. He planted this eternal ache in our hearts to prompt

and prod us to take hold of the eternal life that is found in Jesus. He has put a sense of eternal purpose and destiny in us,
leading us to a relationship with Him.

A true dilemma results from this eternal "itch" that God
puts in the human heart. Nothing that you and I can conceive
provides the ability to "scratch" this itch. The world in which
we live, and the spirit of this age, offer us no ability to satisfy
this yearning for the "everlasting belongingness" that is eternity. Our own mortality militates against this sense of something
eternal within us. The culture that we live in is rushing toward
the latest craze that offers instant gratification. There is some
pleasure in the moment in such indulgence, but nothing that
addresses the real issue.

Many people live their entire lives in the crossfire of this
inner battle. The brain cries out within them for the latest im-
provement or technological advancement, while the heart is
searching for everlasting-ness. The brain and the five senses
may be willing to be surrounded by the fulfillment of their
latest desire, but not the heart. Something inside each human
heart is simply beyond that. We long for something much
more than gadgetry, technology and entertainment. The heart
is aware of the immortal and eternal dimension of life. There
is an inner craving to live in the wonder and beauty that exists
outside of the confines of mere humanity. There is a timeless
realm of life that beckons to us, and while we long to respond,
we don't seem to know how.

People do all sorts of things to attempt to fill the eternal
vacancy that they sense inside their hearts. Every imaginable
sensual fulfillment is explored, and experimentation with all
sorts of drugs, excessive pleasure, work addiction, recreation,
meditation, virtual experiences and an endless list of devices
are employed. All of these experimentations lead us to the
same conclusions: nothing but the life of God within us satis-
fies the inner need to touch the eternal.

God designed us with the need for Him in our own lives
because He loves us and wants His best for us. We cannot live
in harmony with Heaven without God's Spirit living in us.
This divine rhythm of life brought forth by the Holy Spirit's
presence in us is the desire of the Father for us all. We can walk
in a way that fulfills the desires of our heart in this life, and

prepares us to live forever with Him in the life to come. He made us for such a life, and has established the cadence of this life to be followed by His Spirit abiding in us. The Spirit of God enters our hearts to capture our affection and attention, and to lead us into God's destiny and purpose for our lives.

He lives in us as Christians to help us see what truly matters, in each moment and for eternity. The Spirit of God establishes this tempo of life within us, empowering us to fulfill the eternal ache and to make us content in our daily walk with Him.

The Lord made you in His image, *on purpose* and *for a purpose*. His desire is to bring you into a relationship with Him that gives you life as He defines it in all its fullness. Once that connection is made, He works within us to create a rhythm to your life that gives you the deepest enjoyment of the God who made you, the richest fulfillment of His purposes for you, and the love and power to give His life to those around you. He captures our hearts so that we can love Him, be loved by Him and bring others into the love, mercy and grace He died to give them. May your heart beat with the rhythm of Heaven's heart.

ORDER FORM

	Qty.	Price	Total
Rhythm of a Captured Heart	_____	$10.00	_____
		Subtotal	_____
Shipping Add 10% (Minimum of $4.00)			_____
Missouri Residents Add 7.725% Sales Tax			_____
Total Enclosed *(Domestic Orders Only/U.S. Funds)*			_____

Send payment with order to:
Oasis House
PO Box 522
Grandview, MO 64030-0522

Name _____

Address _____

City _____ State _____ Zip _____

Email _____

For quantity discounts and MasterCard/VISA or international orders, call 816-767-8880 or order on our fully secure website: *www.oasishouse.com.*

To contact John Brown
www.johnbrownspen.com
Email: johnbrownspen@gmail.com